ABOUT THE EDITORS

Malcolm MacLachlan is Associate Professor of Psychology and a Fellow of Trinity College Dublin and the Psychological Society of Ireland. He has published extensively on the interplay between culture and health, international aid and development, and embodiment in physical rehabilitation. Recent books include *Cultivating Suicide? Destruction of Self in a Changing Ireland* (with Caroline Smyth and Anthony Clare) and *Cultivating Pluralism: Psychological, Social and Cultural Perspectives on a Changing Ireland* (with Michael O'Connell). He is also the General Series Editor of the "Pressure Points in Irish Society" Series published by The Liffey Press. He is Visiting Clinical Psychologist at Cappagh National Orthopedic Hospital and is currently Chairperson of the National Committee for the Economic and Social Sciences.

Caroline Smyth is a graduate student in the Department of Psychology, Trinity College Dublin. She is currently carrying out research in the area of adolescent suicide and culture change for her PhD. Other research interests include the impact of culture change on mental health and adolescent mental health. She is co-author (with Malcolm MacLachlan and Anthony Clare) of *Cultivating Suicide? Destruction of Self in a Changing Ireland.*

BINGE DRINKING AND YOUTH CULTURE

Alternative Perspectives

Edited by
Malcolm MacLachlan and Caroline Smyth

The Liffey Press

Published by
The Liffey Press
Ashbrook House
10 Main Street
Raheny, Dublin 5, Ireland
www.theliffeypress.com

A catalogue record of this book is
available from the British Library.

ISBN 1-904148-42-5

Printed in the Republic of Ireland by Colour Books Ltd.

CONTENTS

ACKNOWLEDGEMENTS

We would like to thank various people who facilitated the conference in November 2003, which gave rise to this book. Shane Butler of Trinity College Dublin and Adrian Furnham of University College London provided valuable advice and guidance at an early stage, and Laura Mahoney facilitated our use of the Royal Irish Academy as the venue. Elizabeth Yorke, Malcolm George and Chris Searle helped to make the conference happen, while the Advertising Information Group and the Associazione Internazionale Carita Politica, funded and supported the event. We thank the various contributors to this volume who we believe have made it a meaningful and thoughtful contribution to tackling the desperate problem of drinking, especially among young people. Finally, David Givens and Brian Langan have provided the expert, speedy and at all times professional input for which The Liffey Press is now well known.

To moderation, in all things!

Introduction

Chapter 1

BINGE DRINKING:
TOWARDS CONSTRUCTIVE ACTION

Malcolm MacLachlan *and* Caroline Smyth
Department of Psychology, Trinity College Dublin

It is legal to ingest some substances and illegal to ingest others. Such a distinction is predicated on the notion of maintaining social order and personal health. The idea that it is good to consume many substances to a moderate extent, and bad to consume them to excess, is similarly predicated on the idea of maintaining social order and personal health. The way in which we define "drugs" is but one example of how we view such substances — either in the absolute, or along a continuum. Some things one should never take and others one must not take too much of. Alcohol is an especially complex drug. On the one hand, it is often socially prescribed, for religious ceremonies, social lubrication and so on. On the other, it is socially proscribed, before a certain age (except in religious ceremonies), within certain sub-cultural (or other religious) groups and in excess. The do's and don'ts of alcohol use are complex, confusing and, in some respects, possibly self-contradictory. One thing, however, everybody seems to be agreed upon is that binge drinking is bad both for the person doing it and for those affected by its often destructive ripples. Binge drinking is an increasing problem, especially among the young, at least in some countries.

The negative effects of binge drinking include both mental and physical health problems, which in extreme form are self-destructive acts; either slowly through progressive assaults on the physical capacity of the body to maintain functioning, or more rapidly, and dramatically, through a person's attempt to take their own life. There is, however, controversy concerning precisely what constitutes a binge. The need to define a binge arises because alcohol consumption varies along a continuum. For public health reasons it is desirable to indicate to people the level at which drinking becomes problematic. Additional confusion has also arisen as a result of recent research findings which indicate that, aside from social or cultural justifications for alcohol use, its moderate consumption appears to be health giving.

Clearly the term "binge" is not neutral. The Oxford Reference Dictionary defines it as "a period of uncontrolled eating, drinking, etc" and "to go on a spree". The "uncontrolled" certainly resonates with the image of rampaging youth out of control. Yet binge drinking is not an issue confined to the young. Nor is it often uncontrolled. Rather it may be planned, coordinated and keenly anticipated. To define a "binge" as drinking the equivalent of a certain number of units of alcohol in a given time is problematic because some will feel that any such arbitrary figure is an understatement, while others will feel that it is an overstatement. It is also difficult to define what a binge is relative to the normative drinking pattern because drinking patterns vary greatly across cultures, nations and age groups. As a result, we will not align ourselves with a single definition. Instead, we will emphasise the negative consequences which arise from the *pattern of drinking* rather than focus on the controllability, morality or wisdom of it, per se.

Perspectives

This volume does not seek to be a comprehensive review or evaluation of the area; rather, it offers a selection of snapshots from perspectives that we feel have not been sufficiently developed to date. In emphasising the role of youth culture, it also seeks to explore a particular type of binge drinking. The first section of the book, Literature Review, considers the causes, consequences and possible "cures" for binge drinking from a psychosocial perspective. This sets the stage for exploring specific issues. The second section, Differing Perspectives, considers arguments that, on the one hand, alcohol (in moderation) confers health benefits, while on the other, excessive alcohol drinking may facilitate a path to suicide. These could hardly be more contrasting perspectives and, while extremes, nonetheless represent important compass points that people on either side of the "public health – drinks industry" debate sometimes steer their arguments by. The chapter on suicide also provides a link to the next section, Contextualising Consumption. This section provides both quantitative and qualitative analysis of the relationship between youth culture and alcohol consumption. The consumption of alcohol cannot be considered without examining where it happens — the "social spaces" — and what sort of society it happens in. Alcohol consumption has to be grounded in the social contexts in which it occurs. Even when the drinks industry is dominated by multinationals with global perspectives, it is important, in fact perhaps even more important, to consider local reactions to, and constructions of, alcohol consumption. The final section, Debates, highlights some of the issues raised in an Open Forum discussion with a range of contributors.

While the issue of binge drinking is of international relevance, its extremes of occurrence within Ireland offers a particularly valuable "case study" for those interested in the problem. Thus, the latter part of this book explicitly grounds youth culture and binge drinking within the specifically Irish social, economic and cultural context. However, while the patterning of salient variables may take up a particular configuration in the Irish context, relationships between these variables are apparent elsewhere too. As socio-culturally orientated psychologists, we feel that generalisations from one context (country) to another can only validly take place at the level of salient relationships between variables, rather than their specific patterns, because these are always affected by, indeed *products of*, the context that gives rise to them.

While we recognise the need for a strong scientific basis through which the discussion of binge drinking can be informed, we are also acutely aware that the greatest contention regarding binge drinking arises not so much from dispute about the "facts" per se, but about what they mean to the various groups and, more broadly, their implications for society. The viewer is thus also a part of the view, that is to say, the self-interests of different parties frame what they see as being important. So, what are the different viewpoints with regard to binge drinking? Those which jump to mind most readily come from the drinks industry, advertising industry and the public health community (which may be seen to incorporate governmental and civil society interests). Again, most obviously, the drinks manufacturers want to maintain or increase their sales; advertising agencies want to similarly maintain or increase the demand for advertising; and public health interests are concerned with protecting and enhancing the welfare of the general population.

A persuasive public health argument is that increased alcohol consumption (per capita) results in greater levels of social and health problems. A persuasive drinks industry argument is that consumption per capita is too rough a measure, and that it is more meaningful to look at specific subgroups where consumption is particularly problematic, rather than to look at the population as a whole. However, there is an undeniable convenience to this argument for the drinks industry, because the excessive consumption of alcohol by these "problematic subgroups" may well be one of a number of other problems, perhaps grounded in psychological, social, environmental, or other types of disadvantage, and indeed disempowerment, rather than the responsibility of the drinks industry.

The extent to which the advertising industry responds to or creates the desire for excessive alcohol drinking is controversial. Of late there has been much, and in our view quite appropriate, criticism of "lad's ads" which advertise and promote products (e.g. alcopops) targeted specifically at more vulnerable or problematic populations such as adolescents. These forms of advertising often imply an association between consumption and popularity, pleasure and/or sexual success. The advent of advertising promoting responsible drinking is to be welcomed, but many will be suspicious that this is simply to gain favour with advertising standards bodies and governments who have become increasingly critical. The advertising industry seems to, on the one hand, disclaim responsibility for influencing alcohol consumption, while on the other, being able to secure huge advertising contracts from the drinks industry — nice work, if you can get it!

As the chapters within this book amply illustrate, it is widely acknowledged that there is a problem of binge drinking with youth, although more so in some countries than others. The public health argument, that greater consumption creates greater problems, also needs to take account of why rates of alcohol consumption (and binge drinking) vary across nations and cultural groups. In addition, such an account must recognise that alcohol consumption, in moderation, may in fact be beneficial and an important aspect of cultural identity. Of course, "culture" must not be used as a justification or excuse for the undeniably great harms that excessive alcohol consumption can, and does, result in.

The three parties we have isolated above — drinks industry, advertising industry and public health community — are, of course, a simplification of the situation. Governments, for instance, while purporting to have the health of their citizens as a primary concern, are also keen to be seen to promote "individual freedom"; pleased to have massive duty and tax revenues from alcohol; and concerned to appease the multitude of influential lobbyists that the many other vested interests employ. To some extent national governments are however limited in what they can do because excessive alcohol consumption is not a problem bounded by borders — it is a truly international problem and one that requires an internationally coordinated response.

Communication

We believe that in a very modest way, this book represents the recognition of the need for such a response. The conference on which this book is based was funded through the Advertising Information Group (AIG, based in Brussels), which is supported by companies from various industries, including the drinks industry. In agreeing to become involved in this venture, we insisted on (and were unreservedly given) complete control over speakers at that conference and contributions to this book. This is surely a positive sign of openness and represents a willingness to engage in debate. However, just as important as the *content* of this book is the *social context* in which events, such as our conference, occur. There will be those who suggest that doing anything connected to the drinks or advertising industries is to "sell out", and further that these industries simply want an association with "respectable" figures, so as to enhance their own public image (irrespective of its accuracy) and convey the image of genuinely trying to address the issue.

Such strong views are understandable because they concern something that really matters! Binge drinking is both personally and socially destructive. It is appropriate that those who spend their working lives concerned with the effects of alcohol also develop principled positions. Sometimes this may lead such people to wish not to "share a platform" with representatives from the drinks industry for fear of being seen as a "hired gun". While respecting the *convictions* of such "refuseniks", we strongly feel that this is the wrong way to go about realising them. If debate on the issue of binge drinking is justified (and it is), then such debate can only meaningfully take place between people with *opposing* views. Indeed, we have views that are contrary to those of the advertising and drinks industries and may run contrary to those they might like to hear. Nonetheless, we relish the opportunity to express them here, because that is what constitutes constructive debate and it would be churlish not to thank the AIG for their willingness to trust us to do just that, in a constructive way.

In Ireland, where we have learned that you can "only make peace with your enemies", and where the political combatants have been both deadly and extreme, we now have the spectre of people who have tried to kill each other sitting down to talk around the one table. In combating serious social problems, such as binge drinking, there can be no place for self-righteous moralising about the impropriety of "talking to the enemy", and those who fear being outcast by pious colleagues have a responsibility to bring them to the table, for they too are extremists!

A meeting held in 1997 identified the "Dublin Principles" with regard to good practice, and as these relate very much to the discussion above, we note some of their points here. The tenor of the document is the need for mutual co-operation between governments, the drinks industry, researchers and the public health community, and for a coordinated combination of their collective efforts in the management of alcohol consumption.

Regarding the relationship between alcohol and society, the document calls for alcohol policies to be based on good scientific evidence; that appropriate measures be taken to combat irresponsible drinking and "inducements to such drinking"; and that "consistent with the cultural context in which they occur, alcohol policies should reflect a combination of government regulation, industry self-regulation, and individual responsibility" (Principle 1B). It also notes that only the responsible consumption of alcohol ought to be promoted by the drinks industry and that this should be subject to "reasonable" regulation and/or self-regulation. We think that few would disagree that many advertisements fail to conform to this and must therefore question the realism of self-regulation and/or the willingness of governments to coercively intervene.

Culture and Context

Our own interest in editing this book comes from our previous work on how social change may produce significant social problems, such as suicide (Smyth, MacLachlan and Clare, 2003), and how certain cultural constructions of health problems can become disempowering for those who confront them (MacLachlan, 2004). It is well known that the ways in which one group of people view the use of drugs and alcohol can differ quite markedly from how another group of people do so (MacLachlan et al., 1998). The value of considering binge drinking from the perspective of youth culture is that it allows us to understand the sense and meanings that are made out of bingeing, from the perspective of those actually doing it. Just as the reasons for drinking alcohol may vary across cultures and over time (Mandelbaum, 1965), so too do they vary within subcultures. The function and significance of drinking have to be understood: in one context alcohol can be consumed copiously to celebrate matrimony, while in another context it can be consumed copiously to rage against cultural alienation and social change (Brady, 1995).

In a recent review of anthropological contributions to alcohol and drug research, Hunt and Barker (2001) suggest that problem drinking has been too narrowly contextualised:

> Far from viewing problem drinkers or drug users as active agents, immersed in complex social structures, relating to other actors in their social groups, they are still generally viewed as isolated, passive and decontextualized individuals. . . . We seem to find it easier to connect the user with the substance than to see him or her as an actor within a social setting, devising, manipulating and giving meaning to rules, strategies and desires (p. 169).

Biomedical, epidemiological and psychological ideas about alcohol use have considered the "enslaving" of the individual to alcohol, as well as their individual biochemistry, rather than the effects of broader society on their attempts at meaning-making out of alcohol consumption. The latter sections of this book explicitly ground alcohol use in Ireland in a broader socio-political context.

The Irish Situation

Comparative statistics indicate that Ireland is a particularly interesting country for a case study when it comes to binge drinking. Ramstedt and Hope (2003) recently reported that although Ireland has the highest proportion of non-drinkers (at 23 per cent) of the ECAS countries (which include Finland, Sweden, Germany, the UK, France and Italy), it also has the highest alcohol sales per adult, highest reported total alcohol consumption and highest consumption of beer per adult. For both men and women, Ireland has the highest incidence of reported binge drinking at least once a week (at 48 per cent for men and 16 per cent for women), and the highest binge drinking rate per 100 drinking occasions (at 58 per cent for men and 30 per cent for women). Irish men also ominously top the list when it comes to binge drinking, with the resultant behaviour negatively impinging upon each of three separate categories of work/ studies, home life/marriage and friendships, as well as having the highest rates of alcohol being associated with each of the three categories of regretting things being said or done, getting into fights and being in accidents. In most of these cases, Ireland does not just top the tables, but runs away with it. For instance, in comparison to the 11.5 per cent of Irish men who report getting into fights associated with alcohol consumption, only 1.2 per cent of Italian men report doing so, with the closest to Ireland's figure being the UK at 7.5 per cent. Ramstedt and Hope's conclusion that "Ireland has a strikingly high prevalence of binge drinking and alcohol-related harm" (2003, p. 9) seems to be well justified.

In Ireland the Strategic Task Force on Alcohol (2002) has noted the rapid increase in alcohol consumption and its widespread effects encompassing physical and mental health problems, as well as social and financial difficulties. The Task Force has suggested that such difficulties may be attributed to a variety of factors including increased affluence, a relative reduction in alcohol taxation and a massive increase in its availability. One of the concerns in this volume is to consider why excessive periodic consumption is a great problem among Irish youth (although it is in other age brackets too). Dring and Hope (2001), in their study which examined the impact of alcohol advertising on Irish teenagers, argued that the use of celebrity endorsements and sexual imagery were particularly effective for young adults anxious to establish a strong gender identity. In fact, it is interesting to note that their younger age group (12-14 years) expressed more negative and neutral beliefs about alcohol than did their older (15-17 years) group. Both age groups, however, expressed a similar number of positive beliefs and these tended to portray alcohol as conferring feelings of relaxation, happiness and confidence, essentially seeing alcohol as a means towards having fun.

Dring and Hope suggested that the themes emerging from their participants' perceptions of alcohol advertisements included a desirable lifestyle and image, alcohol as social lubrication, sexual attraction, mood enhancement, energy provision, encouragement to drink, learning "how to" drink as though it were a skill, as well as noting the use of humour in adverts and their ignoring of the negative effects of alcohol. Clearly these images are at best only partial and at worst misleading and dangerous. Some of the contributors to this book address the issue of what effects such advertising has. However, there is surely an argument that, regardless of their effects, advertisements should present a realistic image of products, and one that promotes responsible social behaviour. This applies whether one is selling motor cars, dog food or alcopops.

Contributions to this Volume

Following this introductory chapter, our second chapter, by Adrian Furnham, Professor of Psychology at University College London, provides a broad-ranging but concise review of possible "causes, consequences and cures" for binge drinking. Furnham gives a definition of binge drinking and illustrates just why such a definition is problematic. Adopting a psychological perspective, Furnham explores the paths to drinking behaviour and outlines a model for understanding the complex interaction of multiple variables. He notes that personal, social, cultural and economic factors have to be included in any understanding of if, how, and to what extent alcohol consumption occurs.

Furnham also argues that Southern Europeans consume similar amounts of alcohol but they do so in a healthier manner. Perhaps most contentiously, it is argued that attempts to control alcohol through increasing taxation, banning advertising or limiting licensing can, paradoxically, have the effect of actually *increasing* consumption. Based on his review of the literature, he emphasises that education in schools, positive modelling and peer friendships have the strongest and most positive influence on drinking behaviour, while increased taxation or advertising bans are largely ineffective.

The second section of the book, Differing Perspectives, begins with our third chapter by Dr Henk Hendriks, from the TNO Nutrition and Food Research Institute in the Netherlands. He deals with the health aspects of moderate alcohol consumption. This is inevitably also a contentious topic because some in the public health field see it as a justification for the advertising of alcohol, which, in fact, may encourage excessive consumption. It is important to emphasise that Dr Hendriks' chapter in no way suggests that excessive consumption, or in fact even consumption above a very modest level (20-30 grams of alcohol per day, or two to three drinks, for women and men, respectively), has any beneficial effect. However, this chapter remains important for the debate on binge drinking and provides valuable insight into the way in which people construct their own beliefs and values regarding alcohol.

While necessarily more technical than the other chapters in this book, it describes the beneficial effects of moderate consumption, as compared with either excessive consumption or abstinence. Hendriks thus talks of the "optimal" consumption of alcohol, which of course is a challenge to those who promote total abstinence. Reviewing his own research and that of others, Hendriks suggests that the evidence indicates that moderate alcohol consumption reduces mortality from all causes, with its beneficial effects on coronary heart disease, stroke, peripheral artery disease and insulin sensitivity being the most clearly established. However, these relationships are complex and Hendriks is careful to point out, for instance, that while moderate alcohol consumption slightly lowers the risk of ischemic strokes, in heavy drinkers, and especially in binge drinkers, there is a two- to four-fold increased risk of ischemic stroke, further illustrating the complexity of the issue and reflecting the risks inherent in binge drinking.

The fourth chapter, by Dr Justin Brophy, a consultant psychiatrist working in the rural Wicklow Mental Health Services in Ireland, is replete with historical analysis, clinical insight and cultural contextualisation. Dr Brophy considers what might be called the "natural history" of differing consumption patterns in Northern and Southern Europe, and moves on to examine the psychological and cultural background to alcohol use and misuse today. His account amply illustrates how alcohol consumption in Ireland is threaded through multiple facets of personal, and indeed national, identity. Brophy notes a staggering increase in alcohol consumption over a ten-year period, of 50 per cent for spirits and 100 per cent for cider, and this in comparison with an actual decrease in consumption in most other European states. As Brophy argues, alcohol advertising has "skilfully stitched" consumption to gender anxieties among adolescents, whose slower metabolism of alcohol, with its consequent greater proclivity to "drunkenness", undermines the mature identity they seek.

Judicial sanctioning of "extensions" to the opening of public houses juxtaposes with the imprisonment of those who indulge themselves in such commercially sponsored liberalism. Brophy also considers how the retailing of alcohol, whether through themed pubs or up-market off-licences, has increased the "pull" factors to consumption, particularly among the young, who are also victim to the "alcoholisation" of Irish sport. Brophy pointedly poses the question "whether alcohol is part of our culture, or whether our culture is part of the alcohol industry", and who is "minding" this relationship? Rooting alcohol in anxieties associated with globalisation, modernisation and personal identity, Brophy also emphasises that alcohol has direct effects on brain functioning and on mood regulation, arguing that alcohol, in itself, has "lethal potential in that all the social and individual precursors to suicide are potentiated and precipitated by it". While acknowledging a role for legislation, education, pricing, appropriate advertising and so on, Brophy argues that a long-term strategy that has at its heart the desire to confront the collusive denial of the role and effects of alcohol in Irish culture is urgently needed.

The fifth chapter in this book is by Ian McShane, Managing Director of TNS mrbi, a specialised research agency based in Dublin. He reports the findings of an *Irish Times*/TNS mrbi survey of Irish youth carried out in 2003. It questioned youth, between 15 and 24 years, on a wide range of issues, including tobacco consumption, illicit drugs (cannabis, cocaine, ecstasy, heroin and speed), relationships, sexuality, media consumption, diet, politics and religion. This research is important because it provides quantification of the relationships between various facets of youth culture and alcohol consumption. McShane notes that while the majority of 15-17-year-olds drink at home, which is not so different from continental Europe where youngsters are introduced to alcohol in the family context (although see also Brophy's discussion of this issue), there is a different "tone" to Irish drinking behaviour. While younger drinkers are keener on alcopops and cider, McShane asks if they are lured into drinking these by advertising, or if they would likely drink at this age anyway, as a rite of passage. Such a question interfaces culture and advertising, and resonates with other contributions to this book.

Echoing previous research, McShane found that just under half of 15-24-year-olds agreed with the statement "I love the buzz of alcohol" and suggests that this image may be over-sold. Advertising that positions alcohol as only one of several ingredients capable of producing a "good night out" might actually be better able to realise this ambition. McShane's chapter illustrates that liberalisation of attitudes towards alcohol is part of a broader liberalisation of attitudes towards various forms of consumption. However, when asked which people they most admire, the largest proportion opt for their parents, followed by friends and neighbours, and some 70 per cent believe that "Ireland is a good place for young people". The traffic of social change is therefore not all one-way.

Chapter Six is by Dr Paula Mayock, who is a Senior Researcher in the Children's Research Centre, Trinity College Dublin. This chapter places binge drinking in the broader context of the consumption of pleasure among Irish youth. Dr Mayock, while noting the dramatic rise in youth binge drinking, nonetheless argues that what is more problematic than an increase in the quantities consumed is the change in drinking *style*, with heavy episodic drinking to intoxication being a primary feature. Also important is poly-drug use among youth, with alcohol being a "mainstay of *broader psychoactive repertoires*" (italics in the original). These factors, Mayock argues, relate to the dramatic change in lifestyles over the past 20 years, particularly youth lifestyles, with their overwhelming emphasis on individualism and the individual's primacy through the consumption of pleasure, be that in the form of drink, clothing and hedonistic activity, among others. Within a globalised market the drinks industry has developed more diversified products which are marketed as "saying something" about their consumers, and have sought to promote their consumption in contexts where excess is valued over moderation.

Mayock's longitudinal study, using in-depth interviews and focus groups, provides a penetrating and valuable insight regarding the meanings of alcohol consumption that young people construct, and the patterns of normality and social conservatism that binge drinking nestles alongside. For example, most of her participants, including many who drank at an early age and consumed large amounts, did not consider their alcohol or drug use to be unusual or problematic, but merely social or recreational. To address the problem of binge drinking it is necessary to account for the social and economic environment that supports it. Educational initiatives in themselves are of little value and, Mayock argues, we need a "joined-up" approach, not least across different sectors of government, if we are to make a meaningful, wide-ranging and real-world impact on reducing binge drinking. In "giving voice" to those who are a specific focus of this book, the contribution of her chapter is particularly welcome. Mayock's qualitative research does not claim generalisability to other young people, but it does represent an attempt to explicate the sort of personal meanings that larger-scale quantitative studies can only infer.

Debates

The final section of the book, Chapter Seven, recounts many of the issues raised in the Open Forum discussions that followed the presentation of some of the material included in this book. These discussions included contributions from representatives of public relations consultancies, the Advertising Information Group, the Union of Students in Ireland, the National Youth Council, the police, the Association of Secondary Teachers in Ireland, and the Eastern Regional Health Authority, as well as speakers on the day. We let these diverse and constructive comments "speak for themselves". Our own sense of this discussion is that it was critical, honest and constructive, a sense which is perhaps too often lacking in debates regarding the selling of alcohol and the saving of public health.

Conclusions

It is clear that not all contributors to this volume share similar views. Nonetheless, all *do* agree that the pattern of binge drinking commonly seen in Ireland has become a distinctive feature of our "youthscape" and is a major problem that needs to be addressed, and emphatically so. In considering the problem of binge drinking from a number of different perspectives there is a danger of scaling-up the problem and finding so many factors related to its occurrence (from globalisation to plaque), that responsibility for action becomes diffused. However, while there are many vested interests, there are also many opportunities to contribute solutions, although these need to be effectively coordinated by some governmental, or ideally inter-governmental, group specifically dedicated to health-promoting initiatives that interlock across different sectors of society.

It is also important to recognise that, quite simply, the drinks industry sells alcohol and the advertising industry assists them in this, and that they both have a perfect right to do what they do. The public health perspective need not be juxtaposed with a drinks/advertising industry perspective. It is conceivable that binge drinking is bad business for the drinks industry in that, apart from the explicit social and health problems it produces, it also discourages those that might drink from doing so. If drinking in moderation is indeed beneficial, then the public health initiative should be encouraging it! We are not in a position to do the arithmetic, but mass moderate consumption may be more attractive to the drinks industry than a minority consuming excessively, and another minority abstaining altogether.

Without doubt the "squeeze" is now on the drinks industry, and quite rightly so. They, in conjunction with advertisers, have been highly successful in segmenting the alcohol consumption market, and have accordingly come up with designer drinks that give the right "buzz" for the right occasion. While Hendriks's chapter may be seen as grist to the brewer's mill, in fact its emphasis is on "optimal" drinking, and does not give carte blanche to the drinks or advertising industry; rather it strongly indicates the need to convey a healthy context and style of consumption. While the morality of who *should* address the bingeing problem may be debated (endlessly), another way of thinking about the issue is who *can* address it. Of course, we all can, but it is undeniable that the drinks and advertising industries are particularly well positioned to do so and therefore have a responsibility to do so.

We hope that this book is a sign of an increasing openness on behalf of the drinks and advertising industries to enter into a meaningful dialogue about alcohol consumption. Although we have touched on only a few of the salient issues here, there is enough known to make a difference. Beyond the Dublin Principles there needs to be implementation, accountability and social responsibility in a coordinated approach to alcohol consumption.

References

Brady, M. (1995) "Culture in treatment, culture as treatment: A critical appraisal of developments in addiction programmes for indigenous North Americans and Australians". *Social Science and Medicine*, 41, 1487-1498.

Hunt, G. and Barker, J.C. (2001) "Socio-cultural anthropology and alcohol and drug research: Towards a unified theory". *Social Science & Medicine*, 53, 165-188.

The Dublin Principles (1997) (available from the National College of Ireland: www.ncir.ie/info/dubprin/welcome.html).

MacLachlan, M. (2004) "Health, Empowerment & Culture". In M. Murray (ed.), *Critical Health Psychology*. London: Pergamon.

MacLachlan, M., Page, R., Robinson, G.L., Nyirenda, T. and Ali, S. (1998) "Patient's Perceptions of Chamba (Marijuana) Use in Malawi", *Substance Use and Misuse*. 33(6), 1-7.

Mandelbaum, D.G. (1965) "Alcohol and Culture". *Current Anthropology*, 6, 281-294.

Smyth, C.L., MacLachlan, M. and Clare, A. (2003) *Cultivating Suicide? Destruction of Self in a Changing Ireland*. Dublin: The Liffey Press.

Literature Review

Chapter 2

BINGE DRINKING:
CAUSES, CONSEQUENCES AND CURES

Adrian Furnham
Department of Psychology, University College London

Alcohol abuse, especially among the young, is a serious issue. It is all the more so when young people get involved in so-called *binge drinking* which is particularly unhealthy and dangerous. It is particularly problematic when it is associated with criminal, licentious or risky activities and for this reason is to be seen not only as a societal concern but as a health issue more generally. This behaviour may also be associated with other illegal drug taking. In addition, there are any number of societal costs to excessive and binge drinking which range from driving accidents to absenteeism from work to impulsive behaviour and violent crime.

This chapter examines those factors that influence young people in Western, developed countries to use and abuse alcohol. It attempts to briefly examine each of cultural, historical and sociological features that shape a nation's drinking patterns. It also takes a psychological approach in attempting to understand what turns a young person into a non-drinker or a modest, moderate, heavy, secretive or abusive drinker. More importantly, it attempts to examine how social mores, national customs and legal regulation attempt to specify who can or cannot drink alcohol, where, when and how much. A particular focus will be on attempts to control unhealthy drinking (usually with the specific aim of reducing

such behaviour) and more specifically, how to prevent it. Recent research on binge drinking is reviewed and the perceived causes and consequences of binge drinking are examined. There are *two* very clear findings from the myriad of studies on the topic. First, unhealthy drinking is
caused by a multitude of different factors (personal, social, cultural and
economic) that interact to produce individual and national drinking habits and, as a result, an understanding of the issue can only arise from a
multi-causal interpretation. Second, attempts to reduce, regulate and control alcohol intake by governments often ignores the complexities of the
issue and simple-minded attempts at increased taxation, limiting licensing or banning advertising can have unanticipated and paradoxical effects actually doing the opposite of that intended.

What is Binge Drinking?

In Britain an estimated 6.4 million people can be classified as "moderate
to heavy drinkers" and a further 1.8 million people as "very heavy drinkers". We drink less than our grandparents (nearly 25 per cent less than
1901) but more than our parents (121 per cent up on 1951). In Britain we
closely approximate the European average for consumption (Luxem-
bourg, Ireland and Portugal being highest; Finland and Sweden being
lowest). In short, young people are drinking more than they used to. Interestingly, while a third of British 15-year-olds report having been
drunk at aged 13 years or younger, this was true of less than a tenth of
French or Italian children. The greatest consumption occurs among 16-
24-year-olds, who do not drink daily but often at the weekend. Aggre-
gated over a 12-month period the British (along with the Swedes) are
twice as likely to have binge drinking occasions compared to the Italians
and the French.

There are interesting and important national figures on drinking and
changes which have occurred over time. Per capita consumption in litres
of pure alcohol according to recent statistics is shown in Figure 2.1.

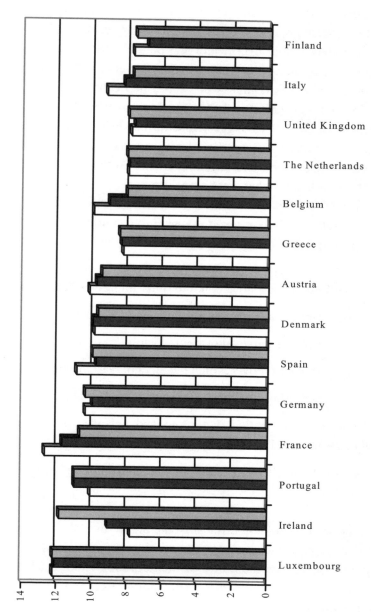

Figure 2.1: European Alcohol Consumption Patterns, 1990–99

At the most simple level binge drinking may be conceptualised as drinking a large quantity of alcohol in a short period of time, usually with the specific aim of getting drunk. There is considerable disagreement, however, among researchers and policy makers as to what, more specifically than this, constitutes binge drinking. The issue most people are rightly concerned about, other than health and possible addiction, is that binge drinking is associated with accidents (Hingson et al., 2003) and irresponsible sexual practices (Dunn et al., 2003) particularly in young people. Wechsler and Kuo (2000) asked students what they thought characterised binge drinking. They suggested six drinks in a row for men and five for women. Interestingly, the students' estimates of binge behaviour changed alongside their own drinking levels. Further, students estimated that a third of their number were binge drinkers.

In academic literature "binge drinking" is usually defined as *five or more alcoholic drinks consumed in one sitting*. Various researchers have objected to this definition with De Jong (2003) outlining three problematic aspects:

- This definition takes no account of other important factors such as:

  o The drinker's weight and height

  o The drinker's personal drinking history

  o The time period over which the alcohol was consumed

  o Whether or not food was consumed with the alcohol

- The idea of intermittent yet prolonged episodes of alcohol abuse ought be included

- The use of cut-off points assumes that consumption below this level is safe.

As can be seen from these criticisms, the failure to include such individual and contextual factors is not only overly simplistic and reductionist in nature, but reduces the utility of the definition itself. Such criticism, however, does not pass without contention. Responding to De Jong (2003), Naimi et al. (2003) noted:

By using specific levels to define binge drinking, we do not mean to imply that consuming up to a certain number of drinks is either safe or desirable. However, while no definition or guideline is perfectly suited to every individual or situation, a single question about binge drinking reliably screens for alcohol problems. Furthermore, binge drinking provides an understandable framework by which to communicate concepts of risk to the general public. Binge drinking is risky because of consuming five or more (or four or more) drinks on a single occasion usually results in intoxication, and almost always in impairment. The link between binge drinking and acute alcohol-related impairment has been demonstrated through three lines of evidence: 1) most binge drinkers report drinking with the intention of getting drunk; 2) drinking at binge levels worsens performance of mental and physical tasks; and 3) binge drinking is statistically associated with adverse outcomes in epidemiologic studies. Therefore, we believe binge drinking is a valuable construct for assessing acute alcohol-related impairment as well as the effectiveness of programmes to prevent its consequences (p. 1636).

Much confusion remains, such that the prestigious *Journal of Studies on Alcohol* set out the following guidance for authors in 2003:

While some contributors have simply used a set number of drinks per drinking occasion to define a binge (e.g. five drinks in a row for men and four drinks in a row for women), others feel that the term "binge" should only be used to describe an extended bout of drinking or other substance use (often operationalised as at least two days) in which the person neglects other activities in order to drink.

In order to avoid the confusion that potentially arises when different clinical phenomena are being described by the same name, the Journal has now adopted a policy that requires the term "binge" to be used in a specific way in accepted manuscripts. According to the policy, the term "binge" should only be used to describe an extended period of time (usually two or more days) during which a person repeatedly administers alcohol or another substance to the point of intoxication, and gives up his/her usual activities and obligations in order to use the substance. It is the combination of prolonged use and the giving up of usual activities that forms the core of the definition of a "binge".

If authors are using the word "binge" to mean something other than the extended period of intoxication with concomitant neglect of activities/obligations as described above, we ask that they change their terminology. Alternative terms for the word "binge" include "heavy drinking"/"heavy use" or "heavy episodic drinking"/"heavy episodic use".

Thus, any effort to understand the phenomenon of binge drinking begins with a definitional problem and so, one researcher may categorise a pattern of behaviour as "binge drinking" while another may not. Indeed, many moderate drinkers may be surprised to find that an average middle-class dinner party may be easily classified as a "binge drinking" session. Nevertheless, for the purposes of this review it should be pointed out that the five drinks per session definition is by far the most widely adhered to by researchers in the area.

Binge Drinking at Universities

Surveys of student drinkers have generally tended to indicate that heavy drinkers tend to be young white males, with this behaviour generally restricted to the weekend. The peak in binge drinking is seen between the ages of 18-22 years with a gradual decrease over time. Importantly, there is no evidence which suggests that heavy drinking in college leads to excessive use later on. In 2000, the Centre for Science in the Public Interest in their Alcohol Policies Project (www.csinet.org/booze/collfact1.htm) reported that 44 per cent of US college students engaged in binge drinking during the two weeks prior to the survey — 51 per cent of males drank five or more drinks in a row, while 40 per cent of females drank four or more drinks in a row. The students who were white, aged 23 or younger, and were residents of a fraternity or sorority were those most likely to engage in this behaviour with those who were binge drinkers in high school being three times more likely to exhibit this behaviour in college.

When reasons for binge drinking were examined, the following reasons for drinking were cited:

- Drinking to get drunk (cited by 47 per cent of those who consumed alcohol)

- Status associated with drinking

- Culture of alcohol consumption on campus

- Peer pressure and academic stress.

These factors suggest various things. First, that drinking is very much a social activity dictated by subcultural norms. Second, that it is often seen as a competitive and instrumental activity rather than a social activity. Third, that young people unused to alcohol or indeed healthy drinking habits may easily be pressured into unhealthy drinking patterns.

With regard to the effects of this behaviour, a higher percentage of binge drinkers than non-binge drinkers reported having experienced alcohol-related problems since the beginning of the school year. Frequent binge drinkers were *21 times* more likely than non-binge drinkers to miss class, fall behind in school work, engage in unplanned sexual activity, not use protection when having sex, damage property, be hurt or injured, drive a car after drinking and get into trouble with campus police.

Not only were the individual students themselves seen to be affected by this behaviour, so too were those around them. As a consequence of another student's drinking, 71 per cent reported that sleep or study was interrupted, 57 per cent had to take care of an intoxicated student, 36 per cent had been insulted or humiliated, 23 per cent had experienced an unwanted sexual encounter, 16 per cent had property damaged, 11 per cent had been pushed, hit or assaulted and 1 per cent had been the victim of a sexual advance, assault or "date rape".

It should be noted that this is American data. The situation in Southern Europe differs: young people still drink, and their consumption of alcohol may be as high as Northern European and American counterparts, but the pattern of their drinking behaviour differs. Thus, the context surrounding the consumption of alcohol and particular patterns of drinking behaviour may be seen to be culture-specific. Tur et al. (2003) studied Spanish adolescents in Mallorca. They found most boys drank at age 18. They drank mostly at weekends, with the average consumption being four drinks of "mild distilled spirits" per drinking day. They also found that adolescents who partook of more physical activity and from homes where mothers had higher educational attainment drank less. In contrast, those whose mothers did not come from the Balearic Islands tended to drink more.

Interestingly, Jones (2003) believes British students are *less* likely than American students to binge because alcohol is more readily available, though he quotes evidence that British students are less likely than American students to accept that their drinking is at problem level. He believes British universities should do at least five things to encourage sensible consumption: hinder special offers or promotional activities which makes alcohol excessively cheap, discourage weekday consumption, encourage the understanding of "normal" consumption levels, counter the climate of approval of drunkenness and tighten up bar/pub admission and service policies to those drunk.

Having carried out extensive work on binge drinking in American students, Wechsler et al. (1998, 2000a, 2000b, 2002) found this behaviour to be widespread. Between 1993 and 2001, approximately 44 per cent of college students were heavy drinkers (defined for men as five or more drinks in a row on at least one occasion in the past two weeks, and for women as four or more drinks). However, drinking behaviour has become increasingly polarised during the past 10 years, with more students abstaining but more students frequently drinking heavily. The percentage of students who abstained from alcohol increased from 16 per cent in 1993 to 19 per cent in 2001, while the percentage of those engaged in frequent heavy drinking rose from 19.7 per cent in 1993 to 22.8 per cent in 2001.

Recently Gill (2002) carried out a comprehensive review of 18 British studies on the drinking behaviour of undergraduates over a 25-year period. She found recorded levels of binge drinking for both males and females varied extensively although it appears that rates are higher among British than American students or indeed the general population as a whole. She noted that binge drinking is seen by this group as a "normal" pattern of consumption, with students paying little attention to government-established sensible drinking guidelines or recommendations.

At the same time, the percentage of non-heavy drinking students decreased from 39.7 per cent in 1993 to 36.3 per cent in 2001, while that of occasional heavy drinkers fell from 24.3 per cent in 1993 to 21.6 per cent in 2001. Students reported getting drunk more frequently in 2001 than in 1993. In 1993, nearly a quarter of students said they became drunk more than three times during the past 30 days; this rate increased to 29.4 per cent in 2001. The percentage of students who said they drank alcohol to get drunk climbed from 39.9 per cent in 1993 to 48.2 per cent in 2001.

Student drinking is thought of as such a serious problem in America that a special issue of the *Journal of Studies on Alcohol* was dedicated to the topic. Here, Baer (2002) highlighted four factors commonly associated with students' heavy drinking:

1. *Family history and parents' behaviour*: Genetics, parents' drinking style and parenting skills

2. *Personality*: Three traits have been consistently investigated — impulsivity/disinhibition; extraversion/socialibility and neuroticism/emotionality.

3. *Drinking motives, alcohol expectances and perceived norms:* Drinking for emotional escape and relief as opposed to drinking for social purposes has been shown to be unhealthy. Expectations of what alcohol does to the self and others is also implicated in unhealthy drinking as are perceived social norms. Note it is the *perception* of how much others drink (and why) not the reality of the situation that is important.

4. *Social affiliation:* This is reasoned to be the most important factor and refers to drinking activities, games and general practices.

But does heavy drinking affect academic performance or perhaps does (poor) academic performance lead to heavy drinking?

One recent study by Paschall and Frasthler (2003) found that heavy drinking did not influence students' grades; however, the authors acknowledge that only longitudinal studies can determine the precise causal relationship and direction of influence. The issue here is essentially that of the direction of causality and the possibility of vicious and virtuous cycles. It is essentially this: is binge drinking a cause or consequence of poor academic performance, that is, do under-performing students turn to unhealthy drinking to cope with their disappointment, or

does binge drinking and its aftermath lead to poor academic performance? Only good longitudinal data can answer the direction of causality
questions though it is likely they are bi-directional.

Possible Causal Factors

All researchers in this area are acutely aware of the fact that alcohol consumption is multi-determined. Consider the substantial list of factors implicated in young people's drinking behaviour:

Issue/Factor Implicated	Author
Adolescent brain chemistry	Spear (2002)
Age began regular drinking	Vik et al. (2000)
Age first time drunk	Hingson et al. (2003)
Alcohol outlet density	Weitzman et al. (2003)
Beliefs about average drinking	Johnston et al. (2003)
Educational attainment	Neumark et al. (2003)
Employment status of consumer	Wu et al. (2003)
Employment status of parents	Lundborg (2003)
Ethnicity	McKinnon et al. (2003)
Expectation and attitudes	Blume et al. (2003)
Less enjoyment in leisure (substance-free activities)	Correia et al. (2003)
Parents willing to supply alcohol	Lundborg (2002)
Party attendance	Harford et al. (2002)
Personality factors	Baer (2002)
Regular church attendance	Vik et al. (2000)
Religion	Luczak et al. (2002)
Same sex sexual experience	Eisenberg and Wechsler (2002)
Socio-economic status	Neumark et al. (2003)

Nearly all researchers find that the variables they are interested in have
some effect but that these effects are moderated by other variables. For
instance, Treno et al. (2003) found alcohol availability (as measured by

outlet density) effects consumption but more so among younger and female adolescents.

One factor that has consistently attracted attention has been parental status and behaviour with research indicating the important role of parents in adolescent drinking behaviour. Turrisi, Wiersma and Hughes (2000) have noted extensive research on the link between teenage drinking and each of parental attitudes and beliefs, awareness of teenage drinking, approval of alcohol consumption, modelling of alcohol consumption, monitoring of children's consumption, parents' own patterns of alcohol consumption, the quality of the parent-child/adolescent relationship and family management practices.

On a positive note, the literature shows the success of using parent-based approaches to early intervention. In their study, Turrisi et al. (ibid) found that the quality of parent-adolescent communication, specifically between mother and teenager, was a good predictor of the latter's drinking. They argued, furthermore, that it is wrong to assume that parents do not have considerable influence over their children even when they are living away from home. They believe their data suggests that there is evidence of the buffering hypothesis, namely, that parents have an important role in *inoculating their offspring* against alcohol abuse. Essentially, this hypothesis suggests that parents can prepare their children to resist the temptation to adopt unhealthy drinking patterns while they remain at home. They do so by example and instruction, thus "inoculating" them against the possible "infection".

In a more recent study, Madon et al. (2003) found that mothers' expectations played an important role in their children's use of alcohol. Family income, parental education and the child's self-esteem were important but there was interesting evidence of self-fulfilling prophecies. Thus if mothers believed their children would drink, they indeed would. Just as it is unwise to totally blame parents for the misdemeanours of their children so too is it unwise to ignore their role as educators, models and providers of financial support. They are therefore important allies in the task of attempting to reduce abusive drinking among young people. Therefore their role both in the investigation of current behaviour and in the development of prevention/educational strategies for the future must be recognised.

Alcohol Advertising to Young People

The standard model employed by those who wish to tackle alcohol abuse often focuses on the restriction or outright banning of what are seen as pro-alcohol messages. Television commercials, it is argued (and maybe even programmes), turn young people into irrational, demanding, uncontrollable "beasts". It encourages them to want and consume products that they do not need, cannot afford and often those which their parents do not wish them to have. Television advertising, according to this model (see Figure 2.2a), creates false, dangerous and expensive wants in the young person. This makes the child pester parents remorselessly with constant demands. Parents try to resist, but this causes conflict, so they give in and buy something they cannot afford, that the child both does not need and may even come to cause harm. Even if you take out the child-parent conflict link the idea remains the same. Television advertising is thus accorded a primary motivational role and hence (according to this line of reasoning) the problem can be solved by banning it. The supposition is that advertising *causes* binge drinking. To believe that advertising *alone* can create wants is incredibly naïve — advertising helps companies satisfy demand at best. Even to the most gullible viewer advertising alone cannot persuade people to buy brands they really do not want.

Figure 2.2a: The Standard Model

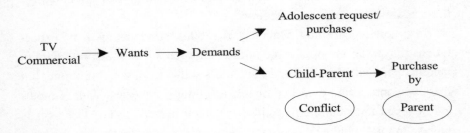

Goldstein (1999) has proposed an alternative model (see Figure 2.2b). Peer and parental influences are known to play a far more important role in purchasing decisions than advertising. Parental responsibility and decision making influence the highly selective nature of attending to the media and to advertising. The multiple meanings and uses of advertising by young people, particularly adolescents, means that television adverts are but one factor. Note that the first model (Figure 2.2a) both ignores the child's peer group and renders the parent *reactive* rather than *proactive*. Even the second model (Figure 2.2b) does not recognise parental values and socialising processes as primary factors. Note also that it is supposed that advertisements not only portray the product but specify how it is to be used. Whilst alcohol products are nearly always portrayed as being consumed socially there is very little evidence that they encourage anything but polite and mature social interaction.

Figure 2.2b: An Alternative Approach

Looking in detail at over 25 studies over a 25-year-period on both advertising and counter-advertising, Saffer (2002) concludes thus:

> Although surveys show that the public supports the idea of alcohol advertising bans, the recent entrance of spirits advertisers in the cable television market has not generated any public concern. Five Organisation for Economic Cooperation and Development countries recently rescinded bans on alcohol advertising. Alternatively, there is an increasing body of literature that demonstrates that alcohol counter-advertising is effective with teenagers and young adults. New restrictions on alcohol advertising might also result in less alcohol counter-advertising. Given these trade-offs, increased counter-advertising, rather than new advertising bans, appears to be the better choice for public policy (p. 180).

Interestingly, and reassuringly, all serious and disinterested reviewers of the literature on the effectiveness of advertising alcohol to young people come to much the same conclusion. Note what Stockdale (2001) concludes after a balanced review:

The evidence for a causal link between portrayals of alcohol in the media and young people's drinking patterns is equivocal. Research suggests that media portrayals are a source of information about alcohol and that they can influence young peoples' worldview and their behavioural choices. But the effects appear to be weak in comparison with familial context and peer relations. Young people learn to drink through a complex interaction of family, peer, and societal influences, including the media.

The ability to drink moderately and responsibly, or to be a non-drinker, implies access to information, credible role models and, when appropriate, "hands-on" experience. However, being healthy and "good" can seem boring — especially if you are young. Experimentation and novel experiences are inextricably part of youth culture and symbolise the perceived invulnerability of youth. Those who seek to promote moderate or minimal alcohol consumption have to appreciate the reasons why young people drink alcohol. It is vital to recognise the excitement and rewards offered by alcohol consumption and other "unhealthy" practices. Demonising alcohol is likely to be counter-productive. The media have a role to play in acknowledging the attractions of alcohol, while not portraying it as the panacea for all ills or the pathway to personal success. In particular, the media have the potential to enrich young people's behavioural repertoire by legitimising a range of drinking "scripts", including both non-drinking and moderate social drinking.

The media have to be seen as merely one element in the portfolio of influences that play a role in young people's lifestyle choices. Media messages alone are unlikely to change behaviour. Moreover, any influence the media exert is likely to be subtle and insidious and to be mediated by the news of those in the young person's immediate family and social circle. These conclusions suggest an agenda for exploiting what power the media do have to enhance young people's quality of life (pp. 231-2).

Furnham (2002) has proposed a model (Figure 2.2c) which suggests that the way parents bring up their children is the central and most powerful causative issue in determining their preferences. This, in turn, influences the child's values, their allowed (and later preferred) media consumption habits and friendship network. This interactive process determines which television programmes are watched and how such messages are perceived and acted upon.

Figure 2.2c: Another Alternative Approach

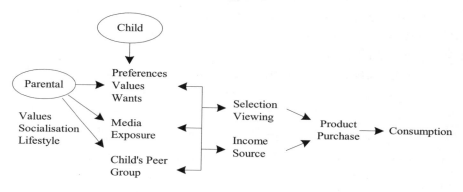

Despite the more inclusive nature of this model, even it leaves out important factors such as whether or not, how much and when parents drink; the drinking habits of the child's friends; and, most importantly, local customs surrounding alcohol consumption.

In order to try to predict a child's desire for or consumption of any particular product, particular clothes or entertainment, three powerful interacting variables have been examined. In order of influence these are:

- *Parental factors*: Their sex, age, values, beliefs and personality, all of which influence parenting style. For many years psychologists have tried to describe different parenting styles (e.g. permissive, authoritarian, authoritative). Using evidence and theories from this research area, Furnham (2000) has proposed that parents with different styles have different values and behaviours and act as very different models. Thus permissive parents will allow children to watch more types of television and have less rules with regard to spending money and drinking alcohol. That is, irrespective of the personality or ability of the child, the way in which they are parental may powerfully influence their outlook, their friendship group as well as their attitude to and experience of alcohol. Parents' social class, personal drinking habits and lifestyle are all crucially important. Every child becomes aware that household rules differ from family to family. Clearly an extraverted, baby-boomer, liberal professional father may be expected to have a very different style from a generation X, unemployed, unmarried mother. These styles impact both directly and indirectly on children's and adolescents' consumer behaviour. Parents' values, beliefs and behaviours are quite simply the most powerful predictors of a young person's knowledge of, and interaction with, the commercial world from the amount of television they are allowed to watch, to how much money they have available to spend and, ultimately, the consumer decisions they will make. In these ways, parents are powerful models of drinking behaviour. No-one denies this. They are also inevitably powerful agents in controlling unhealthy drinking.

- *Peer/friendship groups*: As children move through adolescence their peer groups become all the more influential. Adolescents are very sensitive to peer group expectations, and behavioural and moral norms which lead to inclusion and exclusion. Friends make products fashionable or unfashionable. Most young people are members of various groups simultaneously given their in- and out-of-school activities, though these groups are rarely in major conflict. Shopping is a social act done in groups which strongly prescribes and proscribes the purchase of particular items. Their influence is such that they can and do encourage the purchase of items *not* advertised on television, and/or discourage items that *are* widely advertised. Most importantly, alcohol is consumed socially, often in public places. Adolescent groups differ widely in their drinking style and preferences. And they have a very powerful impact on those in the group, often dictating precisely what, where and how much is drunk.

- *The personality of the young person*: Three aspects of the young person themselves are important in understanding their media consumption and general purchasing behaviour: their *ability*, *personality* and *beliefs* each play a role. Certainly, impulsivity and the sensation-seeking part of extraversion have been implicated in drinking. Less able young people may also not fully comprehend short- as well as long-term consequences of binge drinking. Further, if young people are for one reason or another strong anti-authority or rebellious in their beliefs or values they are likely to reject or challenge the "wisdom" or "instructions" of their elders. For example, impulsive, extraverted young people are more difficult than constrained young people. Their extraversion leads to a craving for excitement and stimulation which in turn influences their social behaviour. It has been demonstrated that personality is a predictor of alcohol consumption, drug taking and sexuality as well as consumer behaviour. The ability of the young person leads them to learn earlier how the economic world works and the meaning of advertising. But it is perhaps the beliefs and values of young people that play a crucial role and it is these that are most strongly shaped by parents.

These three variables (parents, peers and individual personality) are mutually interactive and determine what, where, when, who, with whom and how much they consume. Together with other social, economic and environmental factors (such as neighbourhood and broader cultural context) they influence aspects such as media consumption and purchasing power. With regard to media consumption, adolescents as a group are often enthusiastic consumers of all sorts of media from magazines and television to radio, though they tend to be surprisingly cynical about advertising and marketing in general. While some are rigorously policed by parents in terms of this exposure, others are not. In addition to these more traditional forms of media, the internet now offers a cornucopia of possibilities that is becoming increasingly difficult to monitor. Thus, there is large variability in the advertising to which children and adolescents are exposed and to which they attend. Current generations have been brought up with the media as part of their everyday environment — most adolescents now have personal televisions and/or computers in their bedrooms. As a result, the level of exposure is greater than ever before as an unrelenting stream of information becomes accessible.

A consideration of consumer desires and wants is but one element. Purchasing power — that is, the ability to turn desires and wants into actual behaviour and direct access — is a fundamental component. Young people have available to them various amounts of money which they acquire from three main sources: pocket money/allowances, part-time work and gifts from friends and relatives. By the age of 15 the average British child may have been given £15 to £20 per week to spend, which translates into around £1,000 per annum, and rising fast. This naturally makes them a very serious market and one that is growing. However, there are some major differences to consider. Not only does the amount of disposable income differ, but how or on what the money is spent is an important consideration. Furthermore, there are very dramatic saving and spending differences between adolescents, which has been demonstrated in recent research (Furnham, 1999a).

Figure 2.3: Realistic Model

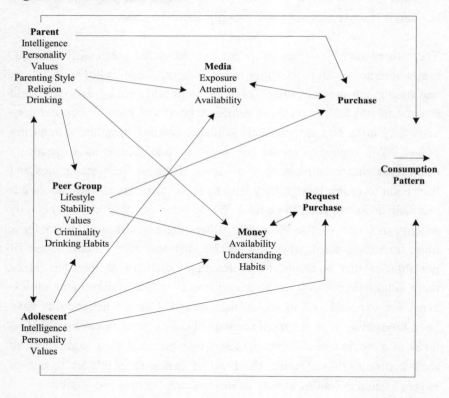

The Influence of Culture

Cultures have been described as wet vs. dry depending on their traditional consumption of alcohol. The questions is, what leads to moderate consumption in wet cultures?

O'Connor (1978) reported the following factors contributing to lowest levels of alcohol problems in wet cultures:

1. The children are exposed to alcohol early in life, within a strong family or religious group.

2. Whatever the beverage, it is served in a much diluted form and in small quantities, with consequent low blood-alcohol levels.

3. The beverages commonly, although not invariably, used by the groups are those containing relatively large amounts of non-alcoholic components, which also give low blood-alcohol levels.

4. The beverage is considered mainly as a food and usually consumed with meals, again with consequent low blood-alcohol levels.

5. Parents present a constant example of moderate drinking.

6. No moral importance is attached to drinking.

7. Drinking is not viewed as a proof of adulthood or virility.

8. Abstinence is not socially acceptable.

9. Excessive drinking or intoxication is not socially acceptable. It is not considered stylish, comical or tolerable.

10. Finally, and perhaps most important, there is wide and usually complete agreement among members of the group on what might be called the ground rules of drinking (O'Connor, 1978, pp. 7-8).

All individuals are located in a socio-legal and cultural context which both prescribes and proscribes drinking behaviour. Some cultures are heavy drinking, others light; some very strict; others lenient. Cultural factors (historical, economic, social) influence many aspects of alcohol consumption: price, outlets, customs. In some cultures binge drinking is almost unknown but in others it is relatively common. Inevitably there are binge drinkers in non-binge drinking cultures and vice versa, but because all aspects of alcohol mythology and consumption are influenced by cultural rules and traditions it is important not to overlook them. Indeed, anthropologists and sociologists may well stress cultural factors while psychologists and psychiatrists stress individual (inter and intra) factors. Both are important and interact in complex ways.

Prevention and Cure

There is much more research about treatment than prevention. The British Cabinet-Office Strategy Unit Interim Analytic Report believes there are essentially four strategies:

- *Education, information and communication* including "sensible drinking messages", health education lessons and by encouraging industry to lead responsible advertising.

- *Controlling supply (availability) and pricing* by regulating suppliers and the levying of tax.

- *Health and treatment services* through the use of occupational health and hospital screening to target people for prevention and treatment.

- *Community safety and criminal justice system* in order to identify, deter, penalise and rehabilitate problem cases.

In toto, the suggestion appears to be that supply and pricing are key factors, which again fails to reflect the multidimensional nature of the issue and the need for education and prevention strategies which match this level of complexity.

Treatments as varied as aversive therapy, hypnosis and psychotherapy are well researched. Over the years a number of proposals to prevent alcohol abuse have been suggested and some tried with varying degrees of success. Prohibition, fiscal controls, licensing controls, advertising bans and controls and education have each at some point been employed. Considering each of these in turn:

- *Prohibition*: History has shown very clearly that this can only succeed where there is widespread popular support. Otherwise attempts to impose it fail, often with paradoxical consequences.

- *Fiscal controls*: This can be related to the alcohol content of drinks or the real price of alcohol production. While some governments vary taxation to keep the price of alcohol at a constant level, consumption is a function of price and sudden, heavy, unpopular taxation can easily lead to illegal or unhealthy home brewing as well as smuggling across borders.

- *Licensing controls*: Making it more difficult to obtain alcohol by reducing licensed retail premises, times at which drink can be served or increasing the legal drinking age. Previous examinations have shown that this appears to increase binge drinking and most now favour the alternative of relaxing restrictions on the number of licensed establishments and acceptable hours of consumption.

- *Advertising bans and controls*: Research on this is difficult and ambiguous with Eastman (1984) noting the paucity of research indicating a strong influence of advertising on alcohol demand.

- *Education*: Most researchers support this approach with Eastman's (1984) conclusion illustrating the point well:

> The best means of prevention in a rational society is through education. If it is to be successful, health education must be continual, it must provide convincing information that can be understood by most of the population, and it must be adequately funded. . . . (pp. 183-4).

Note also the conclusions of Kessel and Walton (1976) on this point:

> Society will continue to generate great numbers of alcoholics. We do not yet know how to prevent this. Even if we did we might well be unwilling to adopt the appropriate measures, since they would very likely limit individual freedom by imposing legal or economic restrictions on the sale and consumption of drink. We already accept, with ill grace, restricted hours of sale and a heavy duty on liquor. If the price to be paid for reducing the number of

alcoholics were to include steps that made it harder or more expensive for the large majority of normal, social drinkers to get a
drink, would that be justifiable? Everyone has to make up his
own mind about this (p. 179).

There are, as one may expect, a wide range of programmes designed
both to prevent and reduce binge drinking. Interestingly, there is now
growing evidence that many alcohol binge drinking problems among
young people (i.e. college students) are resolved without any formal
treatment. This is called "natural reduction" which Vik et al. (2003)
found to occur in around a quarter of the group they studied.

It has been assumed that "life-skills" play a part in the cause, prevention and cure of binge drinking behaviours in young people (Eisen,
Zellman and Murray, 2003). Indeed, Nezlak (1994) found that student
binge drinking related to the quality of their social lives. Using diary research methods they found that occasional or moderate binge drinking
led to a better social life but that high levels led to more social isolation.
Thus, it is in the extreme that binge drinking appears to exert the most
negative effect.

It is well known that prevention is better than cure. Parents, politi-
cians, policy-makers and the general public all welcome attempts to prevent young people in particular having regular public binge drinking sessions and the behaviour that follows. Yet whilst there is general agreement about the desirability of prevention and control there is much disagreement about how best this may be achieved covering economic,
educational and political domains.

While people with very different religious and political persuasions
seem to strongly favour one strategy or another, there remains both a
paucity of good research or disinterested debate on the topic. Many poli-
ticians and pressure groups have focused on advertising as a major cause
of alcohol abuse while at the same time this sector sees advertising bans
as a very simple and cheap way to prevent binge drinking. Control, even
ban, advertising and you prevent the problem, they argue. The data, however, suggests things are not that easy.

Many people are concerned with regulating advertising and therefore
many European countries have set up different codes, guidelines and

laws for advertisers to follow. People are most concerned however about television advertising because studies have shown (Furnham, 2000) that people may spend three to five hours per day watching television, which may over a year mean that they are exposed to literally hundreds of thousands of advertisements. The issue of most concern is advertising aimed specifically at children and adolescents, particularly those of legal drinking age. While most manufacturers have a sensible and seriously self-imposed set of standards and guidelines, parents in particular are concerned about what their children might be persuaded to buy and, for this reason, advertising maintains its central place in the debate.

Teaching Responsible Drinking

How can a society try to ensure that young people use alcohol responsibly and moderately? Peele (1999) argued that alcohol is legally available in most societies throughout the world and, although it may be misused with serious negative consequences, it is more often used in a socially positive, responsible manner. When used in this balanced way, it brings with it significant benefits to health, quality of life and psychological well-being. Given the noted problems with alcohol misuse, however, it is important for the individual to develop skills which facilitate responsible, moderate consumption. Positive use relates to situations of regular, moderate consumption where mixed gender groups of all ages will interact in pleasant, relaxing and socially stimulating contexts. Such patterns of behaviour are illustrated well by those groups which use alcohol almost exclusively in a positive manner. It is this style of drinking that should be valued and emulated.

Considering the important role which has already been outlined for the young person's personality, intellect and values, their parents' values and parenting style, their friends, peer group pressure and product advertising, the question to which researchers and policy makers want an answer is, how do these factors interact to produce sensible or abusive drinking? It is difficult and expensive research but it has been accomplished (Grube and Wallack, 1994; Hops, Davis and Lewin, 1999; Brook, Brook, De la Rosa, Whitman, Johnson and Montoya, 2001). What studies suggest is that parents play a crucial and central role in when, how and why their children drink alcohol. They play a much more powerful long-lasting and inferential role than, say, advertisements. Thus to help ensure that young people adopt sensible and healthy drinking habits it is much more important to focus on parents and education, rather than on trying to prohibit advertising.

Parents model a relationship towards, and pattern of consumption of, alcohol to their children. Parents who abuse alcohol are more likely to have alcohol abusing children than parents who are moderate drinkers. Thus, it is in this interactive, mutual and complex parent-child setting that the "groundwork" for future responsible alcohol consumption is best laid.

Particularly in Europe, alcohol consumption is part of a very long cultural tradition, which dates back to biblical times. Although rates may be high it is rarely associated with ill-health or civil disobedience. In most families children are gradually introduced to alcohol in their early teenage years. Frequently it is "watered down" and served exclusively with food. It is seen to improve conviviality and digestion. Children and adolescents see their parents enjoying food and alcohol together as a natural activity. Not only does this demystify alcohol, but it contextual-ises the behaviour of drinking and through this process of socialisation a more balanced approached may be learned and modelled. Parents need to be more aware of the best way to introduce their children to alcohol. They need to both model and explain the effects of alcohol and the cir-cumstances under which it is best consumed. Naturally children experi-ment with alcohol, often with their friends. However, if children are well socialised by parents, it is unlikely that they will develop "bad habits" with respect to alcohol as a healthier approach and more balanced reper-toire of behaviour will already be available to them.

We know from the American experience that prohibition often has the opposite effect to that intended, that is, it leads to more drinking and particularly unhealthy drinking. We also know that banning alcohol ad-vertising is virtually ineffective.

Alcohol is part of the western diet, much like bread, and is clearly an element to our existence which is here to stay. Young people are social-ised into cultural mores of the traditional national diet, which have often been shown to be very healthy. It is primarily parents who do this but help is needed in the task of raising children in an ever more complex society. Children appear to mature earlier, have more money and be more independent. Parents wisely still try to instil discipline, self-respect and a healthy lifestyle. It is therefore advisable to help parents understand how their behaviour leads to sensible drinking on the part of their children. Through example, instruction, control of the media and monetary allowances they can ensure that their children become responsible young adults not prone to alcohol abuse. Alongside parents, governments, Churches and alcohol manufacturers have the opportunity to influence the one single factor that most powerfully relates to sensible drinking among young people.

Conclusion

Concern over binge drinking among young people is growing — a fact reflected by the number of media reports, public discussion and research papers on the topic. Research has shown quite clearly there are important cultural and national forces that lead to quite different drinking patterns in different countries. Thus whilst Southern Europeans may actually consume as much or indeed more alcohol than Northern Europeans they do it differently and in a healthier manner. This point illustrates the fact that alcohol consumption is multi-determined by cultural, economic, legal, sociological and psychological factors and that alcohol consumption is as much a consequence of these factors as a cause.

For the researcher as much as for the policy maker there are serious problems of definition. There remains disagreement about the quantitative and the qualitative definition of what constitutes a "binge drinking session" as well as a "binge drinker". For some it is five drinks per session but for other it is eight; yet serious researchers in the field insist that even this definition is qualified by other factors such as chronicity of this drinking and general drinking history.

Beyond definitional disagreements there is an overwhelming and almost universally agreed case for education. Education in schools, homes and colleges clearly helps young people understand what it means to drink well and derive pleasure and benefit from drinking. Parents, teachers and other role figures who discuss and model responsible drinking are perhaps the most powerful agents in determining young drinkers' habits and thus are powerful in the move towards prevention. There is now abundant and growing evidence that certain forms of legislation have little or the opposite effect when trying to introduce sensible healthy drinking. Banning television or outdoor (billboard) advertising and increasing taxation on all or selective alcoholic drinks has been shown to have either no effect or indeed result in an increase in consumption. Countries which previously believed in draconian legislation are now turning to much more liberal policies to encourage healthy drinking.

First and foremost, young people, their friends and their parents are primarily responsible for sensible drinking. The alcohol industry, educational institutions and the government also play a part in ensuring the health of young people. Simple political gestures such as banning advertising or doubling tax may gain short-term approval and votes but in the long run are ineffective, leaving us ill-equipped to deal with this societal issue.

References

Abbey, A. (2002). "Alcohol-Related Sexual Assault: A Common Problem among College Students". *Journal of Studies on Alcohol*, Suppl. *14,* 118-128.

Adalbjarnardotti, S. and Rafnisson, F. (2002). "Adolescent anti-social behaviour and substance use. Longitudinal analyses". *Addictive Behaviours, 27,* 227-240.

Baer, J.S. (2002). "Student Factors: Understanding Individual Variation in College Drinking". *Journal of Studies on Alcohol*, Suppl. *14,* 40-53.

Boyd, G. and Faden, V. (2002). "Overview". *Journal of Studies on Alcohol,* Suppl. *14*, 6-12.

Blume, A., Schmaling, K. and Marlatt, A. (2003). "Predictors of change in binge drinking over a 3-month period". *Addictive Behaviours, 28*, 1007-1012.

Borsari, B. and Carey, K. (2000). "Effects of a brief motivational intervention with college student drinkers". *Journal of Consulting and Clinical Psychology, 68*, 728-733.

Brook, J., Brook, D., De la Rosa, M., Whiteman, M., Johnson, E. and Montoya, I. (2001). "Adolescent illegal drug use: The impact of personality, family and environmental factors". *Journal of Behavioural Medicine, 2*, 183-201.

Casswell, S. (1995). "Does alcohol advertising have an impact on the public health?" *Drug and Alcohol Review, 14*, 395-404.

Correia, C., Carey, K., Simons, J. and Borsari, B. (2003). "Relationship between binge drinking and substance free reinforcement inn a sample of college students". *Addictive Behaviours, 28*, 361-368.

Collins, R., Schell, T., Ellickson, R.L. and McCaffrey, D. (2003). "Predictors of beer advertising awareness among eighth graders". *Addiction, 98*, 1297-1306.

Cooper, M.L. (2002). "Alcohol Use and Risky Sexual Behaviour among College Students and Youth: Evaluating the Evidence". *Journal of Studies on Alcohol*, Suppl. *14,* 101-117.

Creyer, E., Kozup, J. and Burton, S. (2002). "An experimental assessment of the effects of two alcoholic beverage health warnings across countries and binge drinking status". *Journal of Consumer Affairs, 36*, 171-202.

Daube, M. (1999). "Pleasure in health promotion". In S. Peele and M. Grant (1999). *Alcohol and Pleasure.* New York: Brunner/Mazel, pp. 37-47.

De Jong, W. (2003). "Definitions of Binge Drinking". *Journal of the American Medical Association*, 289-1635.

De Jong, W. and Langford, L.M. (2002). "A Typology for Campus-Based Alcohol Prevention: Moving toward Environmental Management Strategies". *Journal of Studies on Alcohol*, Suppl. *14,* 140-147.

De Jong, W. (2002). "The Role of Mass Media Campaigns in Reducing High-Risk Drinking among College Students". *Journal of Studies on Alcohol*, Suppl. *14,* 182-192.

Dowdall, G.W. and Wechsler, H. (2002). "Studying College Alcohol Use: Widening the Lens, Sharpening the Focus". *Journal of Studies on Alcohol*, Suppl. *14*, 14-22.

Dunn, M., Bartee, R. and Perko, M. (2003). "Self-reported alcohol use and sexual behaviours in adolescents". *Psychological Reports, 92*, 339-348.

Eastman, C. (1984). *Drink and Drinking Problems.* London: Longman.

Eisen, M., Zellman, G. and Murray, D. (2003). "Evaluating the Lions-Quest 'Skills for Adolescence' drug education program". *Addictive Behaviours, 28*, 883-897.

Eisenberg, A. and Wechsler, H. (2003). "Substance use behaviours among college students with same-sex and opposite-sex experience". *Addictive Behaviours, 28*, 899-913.

Ellickson, P. and Hays, R. (1991). "Antecedents of drinking among young adolescents with different alcohol use histories". *Journal of Studies on Alcohol, 52*, 398-408.

Engs, R. (2001). "Past influences, current issues, future research directions". In E. Houghton and A. Roche. (eds.). *Learning about Drinking.* Brunner Routledge, pp. 147-166.

Furnham, A. (1993). *Reaching for the Counter. The new child consumers: Regulation or Education?* London: Social Affairs Unit.

Furnham, A. (1999) "Economic socialisation". *British Journal of Developmental Psychology, 17*, 585-604.

Furnham, A. (2000). *Children and Advertising: The allegations and the evidence.* London: Saul.

Furnham, A. (2002). *Growing up with advertising.* London: SAU.

Furnham, A., Ingle, H., Gunter, B. and McClelland, A. (1997). "A content analysis of alcohol portrayal and drinking in British television soap operas". *Health Education Research, 12,* 519-529.

Giancola, P. R. (2002). "Alcohol-Related Aggression during the College Years: Theories, Risk Factors and Policy Implications". *Journal of Studies on Alcohol,* Suppl. *14,* 129-138.

Gill, J. (2002). "Reported levels of alcohol consumption and binge drinking within the UK undergraduate student population over the last 25 years". *Alcohol and Alcoholism, 37*, 109-120.

Goldstein, J. (1996) *Children and Advertising: The Research, Advertising and Marketing to Children.* London: Advertising Association.

Gotham, H., Sher, K. and Wood, P. (2003). "Alcohol involvement and development of task completion during young adulthood". *Journal of Studies on Alcohol*, 32-42.

Grant, M. (ed) (1998). *Alcohol and Emerging Markets.* New York: Brunner Mazel.

Grant, M. (1999). "Conclusion". In S. Peele and M. Grant (eds.). *Alcohol and Pleasure.* New York: Brunner Mazel. pp. 403-407.

Grube, J. and Wallack, L. (1994). "Television beer advertising and drinking knowledge, beliefs and intentions among schoolchildren". *American Journal of Public Health, 84,* 254-259.

Haines, M. and Spear, S. (1996). "Changing the perception of the norm". *Journal of American College Health, 45*, 134-139.

Hansen, A., (1988). *The Portrayal of Alcohol in Popular Television Serials.* Centre for Mass Communications Research: University of Leicester.

Harford, T., Wechsler, H. and Seibrug, M. (2002). "Attendance and alcohol use at parties and bars in college". *Journal of Studies on Alcohol,* Suppl. *14,* 727-733.

Heath, D. (2000). *Drinking Occasions: Comparative Perspectives on Alcohol and Culture.* New York: Brunner/Mazel.

Hingson, R., Heeren, T., Zakocs, R., Winter, M. and Wechsler, H. (2003). "Age of first intoxication, heavy drinking, driving after drinking and risk of unintentional injury among US college students". *Journal of Studies on Alcohol,* 23-31.

Hingson, R. W. and Howland, J. (2002). "Comprehensive Community Interventions to Promote Health: Implications for College-Age Drinking Problems". *Journal of Studies on Alcohol,* Suppl. *14,* 226-240.

Hops, H., Davis, B. and Lewin, L. (1999). "The development of alcohol and other substance use: A gender study of family and peer context". *Journal of Studies on Alcohol, 13,* 22-31.

Houghton, E. and Roche, A. (2001). *Learning about Drinking.* New York: Brunner Routledge.

Ingle, H. and Furnham, A. (1996). "Attitudes, knowledge and use of alcohol in university students". *Counselling Psychology Quarterly, 9,* 309-323.

Johnston, K. and White, K. (2003). "Binge-Drinking: A test of the role of group norms in the theory of planned behaviour". *Psychology and Health, 18,* 63-77.

Jones, B.T. (2003). "Alcohol consumption on the campus". *The Psychologist, 16,* 523-525.

Kessel, N. and Walton, H. (1976). *Alcoholism.* Harmondsworth: Penguin.

Larimer, M.E. and Cronce, J.M. (2002). "Identification, Prevention and Treatment: A Review of Individual Focused Strategies to Reduce Problematic Alcohol Consumption by College Students". *Journal of Studies on Alcohol,* Supp.*14,* 148-163.

Lowe, G. (1999). "Drinking behaviour and pleasure across the life span". In S. Peele and M. Grant (eds.). *Alcohol and Pleasure.* New York: Brunner Mazel. pp. 249-267.

Luczak, S., Shea, S., Carr, L., Ting-Kai, L. and Wall, T. (2002). "Binge drinking in Jewish and non-Jewish white college students". *Alcoholism, 26,* 1773-1778.

Lundborg, P. (2002). "Young people and alcohol: An econometric analysis". *Addiction, 97* 1573-1582.

McKinnon, S., O'Rourke, K. and Byrd, R. (2003). "Increased risk of alcohol abuse among college students living on the US-Mexico border". *Journal of American College Health, 51*, 163-167.

Madon, S., Guyll, M., Spoth, R., Cross, S. and Hilbert, S. (2003). "The self-fulfilling influence of mother expectations on children's under-age drinking". *Journal of Personality and Social Psychology, 84*, 1188-1205.

Markowsky, C. and Whitehead, P. (1991). "Advertising and alcohol sales: A legal impact". *Journal of Studies on Alcohol, 52*, 555-567.

Milgram, G. (2000). "Alcohol influences: The Role of family and peers". In E. Houghton and A. Roche (2001) *Learning about Drinking*. New York: Brunner Routledge, pp. 85-107.

Naimi, T., Brewer R., Mokdad, A., Denny, C., Serdula, M. and Marks, J. (2003). "Binge drinking among US adults". *Journal of the American Medical Association, 289*, 70-75.

Neumark, Y., Rahav, G. and Jaffe, D. (2003). "Socio-economic status and binge drinking in Israel". *Drug and Alcohol Dependence, 69,* 15-21.

Nezlek, J., Pilkington, C. and Bilbro, K. (1994). "Moderation in excess: Binge drinking and social interaction among college students". *Journal of Studies on Alcohol*, 53, 342-351.

O'Connor, J. (1998). *The Young Drinkers*. London: Tavistock.

Ogborne, A. and Smart, R. (1980). "Will restrictions on alcohol advertising reduce alcohol consumption?" *British Journal of Addiction, 75*, 293-296.

O'Malley, P.M. and Johnston, L.D. (2002). "Epidemiology of Alcohol and Other Drug Use among American College Students". *Journal of Studies on Alcohol,* Suppl. *14,* 23-39.

Passhall, M. and Freisthler, B. (2003). "Does heavy drinking affect academic performance in college?" *Journal of Studies on Alcohol, 64*, 515-519.

Peele, S. (1999). "Promoting positive drinking". In S. Peele and M. Grant (eds.) *Alcohol and Pleasure*. New York: Brunner Mazel, pp. 375-389.

Peele, S. and Grant, M. (eds). (1999). *Alcohol and Pleasure*. New York: Brunner Mazel.

Perkins, H.W. (2002a). "Social Norms and the Prevention of Alcohol Misuse in Collegiate Contexts". *Journal of Studies on Alcohol,* Suppl. *14*, 164-172.

Perkins, H.W. (2002b). "Surveying the Damage: A review of Research of Consequences of Alcohol Misuse in College Populations". *Journal of Studies on Alcohol,* Suppl. *14*, 91-100.

Presley, C.A., Meilman, P.W. and Leichliter, J.S. (2002). "College Factors that Influence Drinking". *Journal of Studies on Alcohol,* Suppl. *14*, 82-90.

Saffer, H. (2002). "Alcohol Advertising and Youth". *Journal of Studies on Alcohol,* Suppl. *14*, 173-181.

Schippers, G.M., van Aken, M.A., Lammers, S. and Merillas, L. de F. (2001). "Acquiring the competence to drink responsibly". In E. Houghton and A. Roche (eds.). *Learning about Drinking.* New York: Brunner Routledge, pp. 35-55.

Schulenberg, J., O'Malley, R., Bachman, J., Wadsworth, K. and Johnston, L. (1996). "Getting drunk and growing up". *Journal of Studies on Alcohol, 54,* 289-304.

Schulenberg, J. and Maggs, J. (2002). "A developmental perspective in alcohol use and heavy drinking during adolescence and the transition to young adulthood". *Journal of Studies on Alcohol,* Suppl. *14*, 54-70.

Shinfuke, N. (1999). "Japanese Culture and drinking". In S. Peele and M. Grant (eds.). *Alcohol and Pleasure.* New York: Brunner Mazell, pp. 113-119.

Sharpe, J., Raghunathan, T. and Palil, S. (2003). "Examining trajectories of adolescent risk factors as predictors of subsequent high-risk driving behaviour". *Journal of Adolescent Health, 32,* 214-224.

Smart, R. (1988). "Does advertising affect overall consumption: A review of empirical studies". *Journal of Studies on Alcohol, 49,* 314-324.

Smart, R. and Cutler, R. (1976). "The alcohol advertising ban in British Columbia and effects of beverage consumption". *British Journal of Addiction, 71,* 13-21.

Snyder, L. and Blood, D. (1992). "Caution: Alcohol advertising and the Surgeon General's alcohol warnings may have adverse effects on young adults". *Journal of Applied Communication, 2,* 37-53.

Spear, L.P. (2002). "The Adolescent Brain and the College Drinker: Biological Basis of Propensity to Use and Misuse Alcohol". *Journal of Studies on Alcohol,* Suppl. *14*, 91-100.

Steinhausen, H.C., and Metzke, C.W. (2003). "The validity of adolescent types of alcohol use". *Journal of Child Psychology and Psychiatry, 44*, 677-868.

Steinman, K. (2003). "College students' early cessation from episodic heavy drinking". *Journal of American College Health, 51,* 197-204.

Stockdale, J.E. (2001). "The role of the media". In I E. Houghton and A. Roche (eds.). *Learning about Drinking*. New York: Brunner Routledge, pp. 209-241.

Strategy Unit Alcohol Harm Reduction Project (2003). Interim Analytic Report.

Stritzke, W. and Butt, J. (2001). "Motives for not drinking alcohol among Australian adolescents". *Addictive Behaviours, 26*, 633-649.

Toomey, T.L. and Wagenaar, A.C. (2002). "Environmental Policies to Reduce College Drinking: Options and Research Findings". *Journal of Studies on Alcohol,* Suppl. *14*, 193-205.

Treno, A., Grube, J.W. and Martin, S.E. (2003). "Alcohol availability as a predictor of youth drinking and driving". *Alcoholism, 27*, 835-840.

Tur, J.A., Pons, E. and Benito, E. (2003). "Alcohol consumption among school adolescents in Palma de Mallorca". *Alcohol and Alcoholism, 38*, 243-248.

Turrisi, R., Wiersman, K. and Hughes, K. (2000). "Binge-drinking-related consequences in college students: Role of drinking beliefs and mother-teen communication". *Psychology of Addictive Behaviours, 14*, 342-355.

Vik, P., Tate, S. and Carrello, P. (2000). "Detecting college binge drinkers using an extended time frame". *Addictive Behaviours, 25*, 607-612.

Vik, P., Cellucci, T. and Ivers, H. (2003). "Natural reduction of binge drinking among college students". *Addictive Behaviours, 28,* 643-655.

Wagenaar, A.C. and Toomey, T.L. (2002). "Effects of Minimum Drinking Age Laws: Review and Analyses of the Literature from 1960 to 2000". *Journal of Studies on Alcohol,* Suppl. *14*, 206-225.

Wechsler, H., Dowdall, G., Maenner, G., Gledhill-Hoyte, J. and Lee, H. (1998). "Changes in binge drinking and related problems among American college students between 1993-1997". *Journal of American College Health, 47,* 57-68.

Wechsler, H. and Kuo, M. (2000a). "College students define binge drinking and estimate its prevalence". *Journal of American College Health, 49*, 57-69.

Wechsler, H., Lee, J., Kuo, M. and Lee, H. (2000b). "College binge drinking in the 1990's: A continuing problem". *Journal of American College Health, 48*, 199-210.

Wechsler, H., Lee, J.E., Kuo, M., Seibring, M., Nelson, T.F. and Lee, H. (2002). "Trends in College Binge Drinking during a Period of Increased Prevention Efforts: Findings from 4 Harvard School of Public Health College Alcohol Study Surveys, 1993-2001". *Journal of American College Health, 50,* 203-217.

Weitzman, E., Folkman, A., Folkman, M. and Wechsler, H. (2002). "The relationship of alcohol outlet-density to heavy and frequent drinking and drinking-related problems among college students at eight universities". *Health and Place, 9,* 1-6.

Weitzman, E., Nelson, T. and Wechsler, H. (2003). "Taking up binge drinking in college". *Journal of Adolescent Health, 32,* 26-35.

Williams, R., McDermitt, D., Bertrand, L. and Davis, R. (2003). "Parental awareness of adolescent substance use". *Addictive Behaviours, 28,* 803-809.

Wu, L.-T., Schlenger, W. and Galwin, D. (2003). "The relationship between employment and substance use among students aged 12–17". *Journal of Adolescent Health, 32,* 243-248.

Differing Perspectives

Chapter 3

HEALTH ASPECTS OF
MODERATE ALCOHOL CONSUMPTION

F.J. Hendriks

TNO Nutrition and Food Research Institute, The Netherlands

The concept of moderation is widespread and known in relation to a number of behaviours like drinking, eating and pleasure. Recently, the topic of moderate drinking of alcoholic beverages has received a great deal of attention because of the associated health benefits. Despite this interest there is no universally accepted definition of moderate alcohol drinking available (Kalant and Poikolainen, 1999).

Moderate alcohol consumption may be interpreted in many different ways depending on context, e.g. moderate drinking may be defined as not seeking intoxication based on the importance that societies attach to responsible behaviour. Alternatively, moderate drinking may be defined as a typical or average amount drunk, which may vary considerably between cultures and gender and educational levels within cultures. Yet another definition may be more medically motivated, i.e. the amount of alcohol drunk that does not lead to any adverse health effect or social and mental problems.

Numerous studies have shown that moderate drinkers have a lower total mortality due to a reduction in risk for various important diseases. Therefore, moderate drinking may also be defined in terms of optimal drinking, i.e. drinking in an amount and in a specific drinking pattern that has the most beneficial health effect.

Assessing Healthy Drinking Habits

Regardless of the type of definition, the quantification of moderate drinking has proven to be difficult as well. Intakes are still frequently specified as number of "drinks" and "units", which can vary with country, culture and beverage type.

Another factor further complicating the issue is the underreporting that occurs in any dietary questionnaire but probably more so in drinking questionnaires. Therefore, data from population studies may provide a conservative estimate of moderate drinking. Drinking patterns are now recognised as an important factor in determining the risk for diseases and thus are being investigated more intensively. Recent studies have indicated that the frequency of light and moderate drinking is an additional and important factor in health benefits. It is clear, however, that large amounts of alcohol, consumed infrequently, are harmful.

It is important to realise that all data on the relation between moderate alcohol consumption and disease have been obtained from large samples and are therefore presented as an average. Genetic predisposition, other lifestyle factors and special situations like pregnancy and disease will contribute to the overall effect that drinking may have on the individual's health. Therefore, it will be extremely difficult to give advice on an optimal level of intake at the individual level.

Ranges

Scientists have been applying the term moderate drinking for a vast range of alcohol intakes. Similarly, large ranges are observed in the recommended upper limit for problem-free or "sensible" drinking by governmental or learned bodies in various countries. These recommendations vary considerably, but in general, problem-free or "sensible" drinking may be limited up to 30 grams of alcohol on average per day for men and up to 20 grams of alcohol on average per day for women. In addition, it may be sensible to refrain from drinking on one or two days of a given week.

Health Aspects of Drinking Alcohol

Most epidemiological studies have found a curvilinear association be-tween alcohol use and total (all-cause) mortality, that is, death for what-ever reason. Abstainers have a higher mortality than light to moderate drinkers. Moderate alcohol consumption offers protection against risk of death from vascular diseases, diabetes type-2 and offers protection to less life-threatening diseases like kidney and gall stones, and ulcers. Moderate alcohol drinking, on the other hand, may be associated with an increased risk in breast cancer in women.

The higher the level above the moderate drinking range, the higher the total mortality. Alcohol abuse is also known to be a risk factor for alcohol dependence, the various stages of alcoholic liver disease and specific types of malignancies. Binge drinking is a cause of accidental death and of death by alcohol poisoning. Some of these diseases, specifi-cally cardiovascular diseases, have been extensively investigated.

Coronary Heart Disease

Coronary heart disease (CHD) is the leading cause of morbidity and mortality in the Western world. Atherosclerosis is the main cause of CHD. Atherosclerosis, derived from the Greek, refers to the accumula-tion of lipids (athere) and consequently the thickening of the arterial in-tima (sclerosis) that characterises typical instances.

Atherosclerotic plaques develop in different stages. Around the fourth decade of life, fatty streaks convert into fibrous plaques. These fibrous plaques can subsequently change into an atherosclerotic plaque. Following the rupture of the covering dense cap of connective tissue, a thrombus may be formed, which increases the risk of occlusion of the artery and a subsequent heart attack, and thus morbidity and mortality.

The risk of CHD increases with age and is higher in men than in women until old age. In the past decades a number of other risk factors for atherosclerosis and the occurrence of CHD have been described, among which are smoking, hypertension, diabetes mellitus, obesity, physical inactivity, elevated homocysteine level and an unfavourable lipoprotein profile. Considering these factors it is quite clear that lifestyle and diet can influence the risk for CHD.

Epidemiological studies have provided substantial evidence that moderate intake of alcohol is associated with a reduced morbidity and mortality from CHD (Grobbee et al., 1999). Some reports have suggested that beverage type may be an important factor related to risk of the development of coronary heart disease. Red wine has received much attention as a potential contributor to antioxidant activity, because of its natural antioxidant compounds. However, results from observational studies (Rimm et al., 1996), and also from the clinical studies described in this chapter, suggest that all alcoholic drinks are linked with a lower risk. Thus, a substantial portion of the benefit is connected specifically with the alcohol component, rather than with various non-alcohol components present in different types of beverages.

Regarding drinking patterns, Mukamal et al. (2003) in a 12-year follow-up study showed that consuming alcohol between three and four days per week was inversely associated with the risk of myocardial infarction. Neither the type of beverage nor the proportion consumed with meals substantially altered this association. Further, men who increased their alcohol consumption by a moderate amount during the follow-up period had a *decreased* risk of myocardial infarction.

The association between alcohol consumption and CHD is U-shaped (Camargo et al., 1997; Gaziano et al., 2000; Keil et al., 1997), that is, a reduction in the risk of developing CHD is observed in moderate alcohol consumers compared with either non-drinkers or heavy users (i.e. heavy drinkers). At the more extreme end of consumption, the association with total mortality is described as a J-shaped curve, with increased risk of death from accidents, cancer and cerebrovascular disease increasing alongside levels of consumption.

Other Vascular Diseases

The protective effect of moderate drinking on vessels is effective through its effects on atherosclerosis. Therefore, it may be expected that the protective effect of moderate drinking may apply to all artery-related diseases. The diseases that have a strong etiology based on atherosclerosis are stroke, dementia and peripheral artery disease.

Stroke

Stroke is a leading cause of death among adults in industrialised countries. A stroke is a neurological deficit meaning that a loss of brain functioning occurs, for instance, loss of the ability to move or speak. The deficit is of sudden onset, which is caused by a vascular problem in the brain. Two types of vascular problems may occur. The problem may be an occlusion of a vessel, resulting in a brain infarction, which is referred to as an ischemic stroke, or the vascular problem may be a rupture of a vessel resulting in a brain haemorrhage, called haemorrhagic stroke.

Infarctions make up between 80 and 90 per cent of all strokes, whereas haemorrhages only make up about 5 per cent. These types of stroke each have different causes and it is unlikely that alcohol will affect both types in the same way. Population studies in many different countries have shown that light and moderate habitual drinkers have a slightly lower risk of the most commonly occurring type of stroke, which is the ischemic stroke. In heavy drinkers, however, and *especially* in binge drinkers, a two- to four-fold increased risk is observed.

Similar studies have also shown that the risk for the least occurring stroke type, the haemorrhagic stroke, will not be increased by moderate drinking. However heavy drinking again increases risk. This risk appears to be particularly high when drinking is irregular or when drinking is in binges, making this information particularly relevant given the current climate of binge behaviour.

Dementia

Recently, the number of studies on the effects of light to moderate drinking on brain functioning (cognitive performance) and dementia have increased. Some large, well-performed studies suggest that moderate alcohol consumption may reduce the risk of developing dementias of various types, thus indicating some positive effect on specific conditions at least.

Peripheral Artery Disease

The plaques of peripheral artery disease are much more common in the legs than the arms. Many patients with symptoms of peripheral artery disease have multiple blockages. The points of greatest risk are the places where arteries branch into smaller vessels. Rare under age 50, this condition becomes increasingly common with age. About 25 per cent of men over 75 have the problem, but only a quarter exhibit symptoms. Although women also experience peripheral artery disease, it is two to five times more common in men. Men with peripheral artery disease severe enough to cause symptoms have a 15 per cent chance of dying within five years, and a 50 per cent chance of dying within 10 years of the initial diagnosis. The association between alcohol consumption and peripheral artery disease has been investigated in several large studies (Vliegenthart et al., 2002 and Djousse et al., 2000) reporting a protective effect on the incidence of the disease in men and women who drink in the "moderate" range.

Insulin Sensitivity

The results from recent studies on the association between alcohol consumption, insulin resistance (Facchini et al., 1994) and type-2 diabetes mellitus (Conigrave et al., 2001; De Vegt et al., 2002) are very interesting. Resistance to the metabolic actions of insulin is not only associated with type-2 diabetes, but also plays an important role in the pathogenesis of obesity and CVD. Therefore the insulin-sensitising effect of moderate alcohol consumption is another potential intermediary through which alcohol might exert its anti-atherogenic effect.

Other Brain Effects of Alcohol

During the last two decades it has become clear that alcohol does not act as a simple solvent in the brain. Alcohol consumption appears to affect various brain neurotransmitters (those chemical substances which act as messengers within the brain thus facilitating activity) as well as numerous brain receptors (proteins that receive and transfer messages). Moderate alcohol consumption makes people more active; it has enlivening effects. These effects reflect the release of activating neurotransmitters such as dopamine and noradrenaline. Activation is combined with feelings of euphoria (feeling good and confident) and experiencing pleasure (the general "buzz" factor associated with alcohol). The latter effects are mediated by other neurotransmitters such as dopamine and several natural opioids like serotonin and their receptors.

One other aspect of alcohol is its anxiolytic effects. Alcohol effectively reduces anxiety in both social interactions and dangerous situations. These effects are mediated through the neurotransmitter gamma-aminobutyric acid (GABA) and its receptors. However, at higher concentrations (> 50 mg/dL) alcohol also produces loss of muscle coordination, loss of attention and reduced reaction times. These effects contribute to alcohol abuse being one of the major causes of road accidents. At very high blood alcohol concentrations (> 150 mg/dL), GABA and yet another neurotransmitter, glutamate, are affected which may result in temporary memory loss, loss of consciousness and even death, further illustrating the risks inherent in driving while under the influence of alcohol.

Alcoholism

Regular consumption of huge quantities of alcohol, as occurs in alcoholism, alters the reactions of the brain to alcohol. The brain adapts to these regular high alcohol concentrations by changing the concentrations of neurotransmitters and their receptors in the brain (specifically GABA and glutamate). This new balance makes the brain function normally when alcohol is present in the blood. The result of this new balance is, however, that a misbalance occurs when alcohol is not drunk: the person needs alcohol to function normally and the person therefore becomes dependent on alcohol. In other words, the misbalance is responsible for withdrawal symptoms and dependence.

Vascular Effects of Moderate Alcohol Consumption

Arterial Stiffness

Several studies indicate that elevated levels of CVD risk factors are related to atherogenesis and vascular damage, such as stiffer arteries, specifically stiffness of the aorta (the principle artery carrying blood away from the heart to the rest of the body) (Van Popele et al., 2001). In order to investigate the degree of artery stiffness, a method known as pulse-wave velocity (PWV) is used. PWV is a non-invasive parameter of arterial stiffness, and is seen to increase with increasing arterial stiffness.

A cardioprotective effect of moderate alcohol consumption would be reflected in an inverse or U-shaped association between alcohol intake and PWV. A cross-sectional study in Japanese-American middle-aged and older men and women reported that the risk for high aortic PWV was lower among current drinkers and ex-drinkers than among non-drinkers (Namekata et al., 1997). In a follow-up study in middle-aged Japanese men the incidence of aortic stiffness was not related to alcohol intake (Nakanishi et al., 1998); however, contradictory results have been reported in another longitudinal study in Japanese men which suggested that alcohol is an important risk factor for development of aortic stiffness at an intake of more than 16 glasses of alcoholic beverage per week (Nakanishi et al., 2001).

Our research group also investigated the effect of alcohol consumption on PWV, using cross-sectional data of both young adults and middle-aged men and women. An inverse to J-shaped association between alcohol consumption and aortic PWV is reported in cross-sectional studies among postmenopausal women (Sierksma et al., submitted) and among men aged 40 to 80 years of age (Sierksma et al., accepted for publication). The lowest PWV was observed with an alcoholic beverage intake of approximately 7 to 14 glasses per week for both men and women.

These findings generally support the view that *moderate* intake of alcohol may affect vascular elasticity in such a way that it reduces the likelihood of CVD. This is compatible with a vascular protective effect of alcohol that expresses itself well before symptomatic CVD becomes apparent.

Blood Pressure

High blood pressure increases the risk of heart attacks, other heart problems and problems in other organs. A relation between alcohol use and blood pressure has been noted since 1915, when it was reported that French servicemen drinking 2.5 litres of wine or more per day had an increased prevalence of high blood pressure (Lian, 1915) — perhaps unsurprising at such high levels of intake!

More recently, the relationship between alcohol consumption and blood pressure has been extensively investigated in a large number of population studies, including both observational and intervention studies (Keil et al., 1993). These studies have almost uniformly demonstrated that blood pressure increases with increasing levels of alcohol consumption in both men and women. A causal relation is further substantiated by studies showing a fall in blood pressure when heavy drinkers abstain or restrict their alcohol intake (Maheswaran et al., 1992).

Some studies have found that for people who consume alcohol at low levels, blood pressure was not different from or was slightly lower than for those who abstained from alcohol. Yet other studies have suggested that blood pressure increases even at low levels of alcohol consumption. Therefore, there is no certainty as to the exact nature of the association or the level at which increases in blood pressure are seen. It seems likely that a threshold exists at about 30–60 grams of alcohol consumed per day, above which the risk of hypertension increases. This threshold may be lower for women than for men. It has been calculated that above a daily alcohol intake of 30 grams per day, an increment of each 10 grams per day (approximately 1 alcoholic beverage) will increase systolic blood pressure on average by 1-2 mmHg, and diastolic blood pressure by 1 mmHg.

Lipid Metabolism

It is well known that moderate alcohol consumption increases HDL-cholesterol (Gaziano et al., 1993). Based on epidemiological findings it has been estimated that more than 50 per cent of the beneficial effect of alcohol is due to the increase in HDL-cholesterol. In a diet-controlled cross-over study a moderate daily dose of alcohol consumed with evening dinner increased serum HDL-cholesterol after 10 days (Sierksma et al., 2002). The average increase in HDL-cholesterol in middle-aged men and postmenopausal women after three weeks moderate alcohol consumption, in a diet-controlled condition, was about 12 per cent (Van der Gaag et al., 1999; Sierksma et al., 2002). This finding indicates that the increase in HDL-cholesterol is an effect of alcohol.

Conclusions

It is well established that long-term heavy alcohol consumption exerts deleterious effects on the human body, with increased risk to most organs, but primarily to the liver and central nervous system. In addition, there are social problems such as accidents, violence and crime. In addition, infrequent excessive alcohol abuse, such as binge drinking, has adverse effects on health and society. But besides these adverse effects, some beneficial effects exist for moderate alcohol consumption.

The work presented in this chapter provides several plausible biological mechanisms that support the causal association between moderate alcohol consumption and reduced cardiovascular disease risk. These biochemical effects of moderate alcohol consumption include the alcohol-induced increase in HDL-cholesterol and its associated functions predicting a beneficial effect on the construction/synthesis and the degradation of the atherosclerotic plaque. In addition, cross-sectional studies showed an inverse to J-shaped association between aortic stiffness and alcohol consumption. The effect of moderate alcohol intake on insulin sensitivity might indirectly reduce the risk of cardiovascular diseases.

References

Bostom, A.G., Silbershatz, H., Rosenberg, I.H., Selhub, J., D'Agostino, R.B., Wolf, P.A., Jacques, P.F. and Wilson, P.W. (1999). "Nonfasting plasma total homocysteine levels and all-cause and cardiovascular disease mortality in elderly Framingham men and women". *Arch. Int. Med.* 159, 1077-1080.

Camargo, C.A., Stampfer, M.J., Glynn, R.J., Grodstein, F., Gaziano, J.M., Manson, J.E., Buring, J.E. and Hennekens, C.H. (1997). "Moderate alcohol consumption and risk for angina pectoris or myocardial infarction in U.S. male physicians". *Ann. Intern. Med.* 126, 372-375.

Cnop, M., Havel, P.J., Utzschneider, K.M., Carr, D.B., Sinha, M.K., Boyko, E.J., Retzlaff, B.M., Knopp, R.H., Brunzell, J.D. and Kahn, S.E. (2003). "Relationship of adiponectin to body fat distribution, insulin sensitivity and plasma lipoproteins: evidence for independent roles of age and sex". *Diabetologia* 46, 459-469.

Conigrave, K.M., Hu, B.F., Camargo, C.A., Stampfer, M.J., Willet, W.C. and Rimm, E.B. (2001). "A prospective study of drinking patterns in relation to risk of type 2 diabetes among men". *Diabetes* 50, 2390-2395.

De Oliveira e Silva, E.R., Foster, D., McGee Harper, M., Seidman, E., Smith, J.D., Breslow, J.L. and Brinton, E.A. (2000). "Alcohol consumption raises HDL cholesterol levels by increasing the transport rate of apolipoproteins A-I and A-II". *Circulation* 102, 2347-2352.

De Vegt, F., Dekker, J.M., Groeneveld, W.J., Nijpels, G., Stehouwer, C.D., Bouter, L.M. and Heine, R.J. (2002). "Moderate alcohol consumption is associated with lower risk for incident diabetes and mortality: the Hoorn Study". *Diabetes Res. Clin. Prac.* 57, 53-60.

Dimmitt, S.B., Rakic, V., Puddey, I.B., Baker, R., Oostryck, R., Adams, M.J., Chesterman, C.M., Burke, V. and Beilin, L.J. (1998). "The effects of alcohol on coagulation and fibrinolytic factors: a controlled trial". *Blood Coagul. Fibrinolysis* 9, 39-45.

Djousse, L., Levy. D., Murabito, J.M., Cupples, L.A., Ellison, R.C. (2000). "Alcohol consumption and risk of intermittent claudication in the Framingham Heart Study". *Circulation* 102, 3092-3097.

Facchini, F., Chen, Y.D. and Reaven, G.M. (1994). "Light-to-moderate alcohol intake is associated with enhanced insulin sensitivity". *Diabetes Care* 17, 115-119.

Folsom, A.R., Nieto, F.J., McGovern, P.G., Tsai, M.Y., Malinow, M.R., Eckfeldt, J.H., Hess, D.L. and Davis, C.E. (1998). "Prospective study of coronary heart disease incidence in relation to fasting total homocysteine, related genetic polymorphisms, and B vitamins: the Atherosclerosis Risk in Communities (ARIC) study". *Circulation* 98, 204-210.

Gaziano, J.M., Buring, J.E., Breslow, J.L., Goldhaber, S.Z., Rosner, B., VanDenburgh, M., Willett, W. and Hennekens, C.H. (1993). "Moderate alcohol intake, increased levels of high-density lipoprotein and its subfractions, and decreased risk of myocardial infarction". *N. Engl. J. Med.* 329, 1829-1834.

Goldberg, C.S., Tall, A.R. and Krumholz, S. (1984). "Acute inhibition of hepatic lipase and increase in plasma lipoproteins after alcohol intake". *J. Lipid Res.* 25, 714-720.

Grobbee, D.E., Rimm, E.B., Keil, U. and Renaud, S. (1999). "Alcohol and the cardiovascular system". In *Health Issues Related to alcohol Consumption* (ed McDonald IE), pp .125-179. Blackwell Science, ILSI Europe.

Hendriks, H.F.J., Veenstra, J., Velthuis-te Wierik, E.J.M., Schaafsma, G. and Kluft, C. (1994). "Effect of moderate dose of alcohol with evening meal on fibrinolytic factors".*BMJ* 308, 1003-1006.

Hendriks, H.F.J. and Van der Gaag, M.S. (1998). "Alcohol, coagulation and fibrinolysis". *Novartis Found Symp.* 216, 111-120.

Hotta, K., Funahashi, T., Bodkin, N.L., Ortmeyer, H.K., Arita, Y., Hansen, B.C. and Matsuzawa, Y. (2001). "Circulating concentrations of the adipocyte protein adiponectin are decreased in parallel with reduced insulin sensitivity during the progression to type 2 diabetes in rhesus monkeys". *Diabetes* 50, 1126-1133.

Imai, Y., Morita, H., Kurihara, H., Sugiyama, T., Kato, N., Ebihara, A., Hamada, C., Kurihara, Y., Shindo, T., Oh-hashi, Y. and Yazaki, Y. (2000). "Evidence for association between paraoxonase gene polymorphisms and atherosclerotic diseases". *Atherosclerosis* 149, 435-442.

Kalant, H., Poikolainen, K. (1999). "Moderate Drinking: Concepts, definitions and public health significance". In *Health Issues Related to Alcohol Consumption* (ed., MacDonald. I.), pp. 1-27. Blackwell Science, ILSI Europe.

Keil, U., Swales, J.D. and Grobbee, D.E. (1993b). "Alcohol intake and its relation to hypertension". In *Health Issues Related to Alcohol Consumption* (ed. Verschuren. P.M.), pp. 17-42. Blackwell Science, ILSI Europe.

Koenig, W., Sund, M., Fröhlich, M., Fischer, H.G., Lowel, H., Doring, A., Hutchinson, W.L. and Pepys, M.B. (1999). "C-Reactive protein, a sensitive marker of inflammation, predicts future risk of coronary heart disease in initially healthy middle-aged men: results from the MONICA (Monitoring Trends and Determinants in Cardiovascular Disease) Augsburg Cohort Study, 1984 to 1992". *Circulation* 99, 237-42.

Leus, F.R., Wittekoek, M.E., Prins, J., Kastelein, J.J. and Voorbij, H.A. (2000). "Paraoxonase gene polymorphisms are associated with carotid arterial wall thickness in subjects with familial hypercholesterolemia". *Atherosclerosis* 149, 371-377.

Mackness, M.I. and Durrington, P.N. (1995). "HDL, its enzymes and its potential to influence lipid peroxidation". *Atherosclerosis* 115, 243-253.

Mackness, M.I., Arrol, A., Mackness, B. and Durrington, P.N. (1997). "Alloenzymes of paraoxonase and effectiveness of high-density lipoproteins in protecting low-density lipoprotein against lipid peroxidation". *Lancet* 349, 851-852.

Maheswaran, R., Beevers, M. and Beevers, D.G. (1992). "Effectiveness of advice to reduce alcohol consumption in hypertensive patients". *Hypertension* 19, 79-84.

Mukamal, K.J., Conigrave, K.M., Mittleman, M.A., Camargo, C.A. Jr., Stampfer, M.J., Willett, W.C. and Rimm, E.B. (2003). "Roles of drinking pattern and type of alcohol consumed in coronary heart disease in men". *N. Engl. J. Med* 348, 109-118.

Nakanishi, N., Suzuki, K., Kawashimo, H., Nakamura, K. and Tatara, K. (1998). "Risk factors for the incidence of aortic stiffness by serial aortic pulse wave velocity measurement in middle-aged Japanese men". *Environ. Health Prev. Med.* 3, 168-174.

Nakanishi, N., Kawashimo, H., Nakamura, K., Suzuki, K., Yoshida, H., Uzura, S. and Tatara, K. (2001). "Association of alcohol consumption with increase in aortic stiffness: a 9-year longitudinal study in middle-aged Japanese men". *Ind. Health* 39, 24-28.

Namekata, T., Moore, D., Suzuki, K., Mori, M., Hatano, S., Hayashi, C., Abe, N. and Hasegawa, M. (1997). "A study of the association between the aortic pulse wave velocity and atherosclerotic risk factors among Japanese Americans in Seattle, U.S.A." *Nippon Koshu Eisei Zasshi* 44, 942-951.

Nishiwaki, M., Ishikawa, T., Ito, T., Shige, H., Tomiyasu, K., Nakajima, K., Kondo, K., Hashimoto, H., Saitoh, K. and Manabe, M. (1994). "Effects of alcohol on lipoprotein lipase, hepatic lipase, cholesteryl ester transfer protein, and lecithin:cholesterol acyltransferase in high-density lipoprotein cholesterol elevation". *Atherosclerosis* 111:99-109.

Ridker, P.M., Buring, J.E., Shih, J., Matias, M. and Hennekens, C.H. (1998). "Prospective study of C-reactive protein and the risk of future cardiovascular events among apparently healthy women". *Circulation.* 98, 731-733.

Rimm, E.B., Klatsky, A., Grobbee, D.E. and Stampfer, M.J. (1996). "Review of moderate alcohol consumption and reduced risk of coronary heart disease: is the effect due to beer, wine, or spirits". *BMJ.* 312, 731-736.

Sierksma, A., Van der Gaag, M.S., Schaafsma, G., Kluft, C., Bakker, M. and Hendriks, H.F.J. (2001) "Moderate alcohol consumption and fibrinolytic factors of pre- and postmenopausal women". *Nutrition Research.* 21, 171-181.

Sierksma, A., Van der Gaag, M.S., Kluft, C. and Hendriks, H.F.J. (2002). "Moderate alcohol consumption reduces plasma C-reactive protein and fibrinogen levels; a randomized, diet-controlled intervention study". *Eur. J. Clin. Nutr.* 56, 1130-1136.

Sierksma, A, Patel, H, Ouchi, N, Kihara, S, Funahashi, T, Heine, R.J., Grobbee, D.J., Kluft, C, Hendriks, H.F.J. (2004). "Effect of moderate alcohol consumption on adiponectin, tumor necrosis factor-α , and insulin sensitivity". *Diabetes Care* 27, 184-189.

Sierksma, A, Lebrun, C.E.I., Van der Schouw, Y.T., Grobbee, D.E., Lamberts, S.W.J., Hendriks, H.F.J., Bots, M.L. (2004). "Alcohol consumption in relation to aortic stiffness and aortic wave reflections: a cross-sectional study in healthy postmenopausal women". *Arterioscler Thromb Vasc Biol.* 24: 342-348.

Sierksma, A, Muller, M., Van der Schouw, Y.T., Grobbee, D.E., Hendriks, H.F.J., Bots, M.L. (2004). "Alcohol consumption and arterial stiffness in men". *J. of Hypertension* 22, 357-362.

Stampfer, M.J., Colditz, G.A., Willett, W.C., Speizer, F.E. and Hennekens, C.H. (1988). "A prospective study of moderate alcohol consumption and the risk of coronary disease and stroke in women". *N. Engl. J. Med.* 319,267-273.

Van der Gaag, M.S., Van Tol, A., Scheek, L.M., James, R.W., Urgert, R., Schaafsma, G. and Hendriks, H.F.J. (1999). "Daily moderate alcohol consumption increases serum paraoxonase activity; a diet-controlled, randomised intervention study in middle-aged men". *Atherosclerosis* 147, 405-410.

Van der Gaag, M.S., Ubbink, J.B., Sillanaukee, P., Nikkari, S. and Hendriks, H.F.J. (2000). "Effect of consumption of red wine, spirits, and beer on serum homocysteine". *Lancet* 355, 1522.

Van der Gaag, M.S., Van Tol, A., Vermunt, S.H.F., Scheek, L.M., Schaafsma, G. and Hendriks, H.F.J. (2001). "Alcohol consumption stimulates early steps in reverse cholesterol transport". *J. Lipid Res.* 42:2077-2083.

Van Popele, N.M., Grobbee, D.E., Bots, M.L., Asmar, R., Topouchian, J., Reneman, R.S., Hoeks, A.P., Van der Kuip, D.A., Hofman, A. and Witteman, J.C. (2001). "Association between arterial stiffness and atherosclerosis: the Rotterdam Study". *Stroke* 32:454-460.

Vliegenthart, R., Geleijnse, J.M., Hofman, A., Meijer, W.T., van Rooij, F.J., Grobbee, D.E., Witteman, J.C. (2002). "Alcohol consumption and risk of peripheral arterial disease: the Rotterdam study". *Am. J. Epidemiol.* 155, 332-338.

Chapter 4

ALCOHOL, CULTURE AND SUICIDE IN IRELAND: EXPLORING THE CONNECTIONS

Justin Brophy
Wicklow Mental Health Services, Ireland

Alcohol has longstanding and important cultural roles in Irish society. It has, however, become a major problem in recent times broaching Hogarthian proportions which threatens the fabric of civic and social order. Suicide is a more recent but growing problem and in this chapter I intend to explicate the connection between alcohol and suicide in Ireland. I will begin by exploring the reasons for and functions of alcohol use and misuse from both a psychological and cultural viewpoint. I will attempt to outline some of the complexity surrounding the psychological functions of alcohol at the level of both the individual and society. Then I will examine the cultural phenomenology and uses of alcohol consumption in Ireland, from both historical and contemporary perspectives, looking especially at the changes that have occurred in recent times. I also intend to discuss patterns of misuse and the risks and consequences that arise from such behaviour. In addition, the general evidence directly linking suicide and alcohol misuse is considered. That which is specific to Ireland is presented and the basis for links between the increase in alcohol consumption and suicide rates in Ireland are set out. I conclude the chapter with an examination of possibilities of changing misuse patterns, with the emphasis placed on steps that might reduce

Ireland's suicide rate, within the overall limitations and possibilities of our cultural circumstances.

We in Ireland are in denial and paralysis in response to our alcohol problem, partly because of our personal and institutional complicity, however venial, and partly because of the extent of manipulation and infiltration by commercial interests of our attitudes and behaviour. The extent of this denial and the rationalisations that accompany it cannot be overstated. In attempting to offer explanations for this state of affairs in this chapter I am fearful of perpetuating or creating further externalising, blaming myths. Let me be clear, therefore, at the outset by stating my view that the solution to the appalling extent of our drinking problem in Ireland lies within us as individuals, citizens and interdependent social agents. Institutional, structural or societal measures can only be effective if we accept this starting point and face our personal responsibilities. That is not to say that this principle should then be used by commercial interests to resist and undermine their equally burdensome responsibilities to accept structural limits.

That said, I freely acknowledge that alcohol has a cultural value and use, and that I am not prohibitionist in principle. I enjoy a drink and believe others can too. Because I hold this view I find the arguments for proper use so compelling, so that these freedoms and enjoyments can continue to be exercised. The reader will have to adjudge, however, if the logic of my compromise is too much, and where for themselves the balance should lie between restriction and availability.

Cultural Differences in Alcohol Consumption

Culture is important. Most evidence indicates that it is the collection of beliefs, attitudes and norms which surround alcohol, rather than absolute consumption levels themselves, that are very powerful in either causing or preventing alcohol-related problems. While my primary interest is in the medical and psychiatric aspects of alcohol consumption, it is important to note that the medical risk–benefit equation of alcohol is less influential in the absence of some understanding of culture and behaviour, and for this reason I wish to outline the various cultural roles of alcohol and alcohol's role in culture. I have no academic background in cultural studies, and consequently I base my observations as a clinician dealing daily with persons with alcohol-related problems and as an Irish person who has lived through some of what I report.

Contrasts are frequently drawn between Northern and Southern European patterns of alcohol consumption. Recent work summarises much of the evidence (Ramstedt and Hope, 2002). Irish adults are currently among the highest consumers of alcohol in Europe, at 14.2 litres per adult. It is important to note with regard to these figures that many in Ireland do not drink alcohol at all. From the 1970s until the 1990s, estimates from various surveys revealed abstention rates of 20-25 per cent among men and 30 per cent among women. In 1998 the estimated proportion of non-drinkers was 14 per cent for men and 19 per cent of women. Few people in Ireland drink every day, only 1.6 per cent of men and 0.2 per cent of women, with daily drinking less common in Ireland than in other surveyed European countries among both men and women. Considering the high proportion of non-drinkers, these figures suggest that those who drink in Ireland drink fairly often. Mediterranean people's consumption until recently was higher overall in grams of alcohol per capita. Moreover, this consumption is associated with higher direct physical health costs, particularly rates of death from cirrhosis of the liver, but with lower social costs (Ramstedt, 2001a; Ramstedt, 2002).

We, like our UK counterparts, binge much more, 48 per cent of men at least once a week and 16 per cent among women — rates three to four times higher than those of other countries. Of 100 drinking events, 58 end in binge drinking for men, while for women this figure is somewhat lower at 30 out of 100. Binge drinking is thus the norm among men and occurs in about a third of the drinking occasions of women. This pattern seems to yield significantly more misery and social chaos than in other nations (Ramstedt and Hope, 2002). Bingeing is defined variously around the quantity consumed during a given period. However this approach does not sufficiently address issues of the intent, style and outcome of the consumption behaviour regardless of volumes. Essentially, for my purposes, bingeing connotes episodic drinking of sufficient alcohol to effect the outcome of intoxication of rapid onset, and for which control of the rate of consumption is initially wilfully and then drunkenly suspended for periods lasting hours to months. The effect sought is

primarily stimulation and disinhibition rather than relaxation and seda-
tion. So why, when the high cost of this behaviour is known, do we continue to engage in this pattern of drinking?

The reasons for this difference are the source of much speculation
but still little agreement. Firstly, it cannot be overstated that no matter
what the background explanatory hypotheses, the responsibility around
bingeing always remains with the individual. No policy, regulation, legislation or remedy can undermine this crucial principle. In looking first at
natural patterns that might mirror and explain the contrasting phenomena
and cultural configurations of excessive consumption between Northern
and Southern European peoples, I will first turn to the rhythms of nature
as a source for speculation. Biological, cultural and economic calendars
that were once more tightly linked may have contributed to these differing predilections across Europe.

Episodic heavy (binge) drinking, as it exists in Ireland and Britain,
echoes seasonal ebbs and flows in bounty of the ancient native agrarian
climate and economy. Periods of scarcity and hardship facilitate voluntary, economic or penitential abstemiousness. These are followed by periods of excess, celebrating the seasonal bounty and fostering social encounters. Alcohol consumption patterns perhaps echo, mark and become
implicated in these sequences and extremes of reward and punishment.
Such cycles set by environmental imperatives of hunger and feasting,
imposing isolation or communal activity, linked to courtship and other
social occasions like markets or cultural gatherings, and accompanied by
episodic heavy drinking or abstinence, are plausible historic backdrops
and possible formative influences to this pattern which lingers enduringly to the present. In such a schema, intensities of privation or excess
beget their opposites; loss-of-control drinking is a consequence of episodic rigorous abstention. This is a partial hypothesis at best, but any
candid resident of Galway city will attest to this one manifestation of this
phenomenon, the indulgences of race week and the spiritual purgation of
the Redemptorist Novena being met annually with equal and un-
contradictory enthusiasm!

In Mediterranean cultures, where regular daily drinking is the norm,
it is perhaps the climate and seasons being less astringent which beget a
more regular, less dipsomaniac consumption of alcohol. Their ancient

Gods may be considered more unfailingly bounteous in this respect. In contrast, ours are more exacting, and perhaps have engendered more ascetic but also more extravagant behaviour around alcohol. Wine is also easier to store, making the practicalities of Mediterranean consumption a more uncomplicated process. Importantly, drinking is also differently socialised in these Mediterranean cultures, where alcohol is mainly consumed as wine. It is consumed in settings such as family meals and cafes and restaurants where groups of both genders and differing ages all participate. Even alcohol-dependent persons eschew drunkenness, and more effectively conceal their problem with quiet, daylong drinking. There, general alcohol use is more behaviourally benign, resulting in far fewer social problems.

This is in marked contrast to Ireland. Here social encounters are often devoted exclusively to drinking. No-one seems to intentionally eat, we often drink standing up, and individuals within groups often compete to see who'll get drunk first. The link between family gatherings and the consumption of alcohol also appears to be configured differently compared with southern Europe. Here, families as a unit go to the pub mainly on Sundays, but these excursions are not primarily about "family time", and are more to do with legitimating parental (mainly paternal) drinking continuing from Friday through to Sunday. For many children it is the only time with their father in the week, for women the only joint outing with their husband or opportunity to level up the consumption scores. Many children may not see their parents routinely drinking, but not infrequently can see them drunk at special festive events. Family days, such as those around Christmas, after Easter or Saint Patrick's Day, are often celebrated in the pub, not the home. Moreover, these occasions, and many other moments of transition, like exam result celebrations, christenings and weddings (indeed, almost any "traditional" setting), themselves provide opportunities for minors to experiment with alcohol. For many, it forms their introduction to it, and forever establishes the powerfully imprinted link between celebration, consumption and intoxication. This is quite unlike the "wine cultures", where exposure is gradual, supervised and not associated with drunkenness.

One emerging irony is that people in Ireland (especially the more affluent strata) are increasingly adopting Mediterranean alcohol lifestyles, as wine sales confirm. This is partly due to European contact and influence, partly marketing, and partly the misguided notion originating from public health influence that it is a "healthier" option. All the evidence suggests, however, that it is not a switch; although wine itself has been embraced with gusto, the cultural context of its consumption has not been as readily adopted. We still continue our traditional pattern, bingeing when the opportunity arises. This is, of course, the worst of both worlds from a health perspective.

Psychological Aspects of Alcohol Consumption

Turning now to psychological functions, the question of why humans drink alcohol arises. There are several mundane uses to which alcohol is regularly put. These make use of basic pharmacological properties and produce relatively predictable effects and all at accessible, modest doses and cost. These uses include lowering anxiety, taking advantage of the sedative effects; mild euphoria, increasing self-esteem and confidence; releasing reticence, affording escape from inhibitions; and amnesia through increasing intoxication, mitigating the burdens of memory. We also use it to obtain oblivion, the precise psychological function of which is unclear, but important nonetheless. Perhaps it is the simple (albeit temporary) escape from our greatest, but sometimes most overbearing endowment, consciousness. We seek, in particular, escape from the unbearably painful parts of reality.

There are other psychological aspects of the purposes of excess consumption. Alcohol, like all intoxicants, sub-serves additional, more complex but perhaps also controversial functions. These include accessing primitive and intense mental states that connect to more reserved personal and social agendas. To this extent, alcohol functions to provide an opportunity for connecting with our Unconscious in the Jungian sense of the term.

The Unconscious, among its myriad facets, is the domain of our disguised powerful feelings and motivations. When we need to "touch base" with our deeper selves from time to time, alcohol is a popular and "permitted" mediating agent. Alcohol intoxication can engender powerful personal experiences and introspections that seem otherwise inaccessible. It facilitates a link to this elusive, supra-ordinate domain, the domain of self-revelation and occasional truth — *in vino veritas*. For my purpose here, it is important to note that in this sometimes distorting and shaming mirror of truth, the possibility of suicide is sometimes reflected and enacted.

Such experiences can be considered encounters with the polarised and amplified aspects of our good and bad "selves", our personal and collective Gods and Demons. While most often we seek the good self, quite regularly we find also the bad. First, I will consider the good, or "divine" aspect.

On the "divine" facets of this experience, alcohol is used in two important ways. Firstly, it is used to tap into important forces of creativity. Artists and other creative persons often use alcohol to kick-start or maintain inspiration — "to bring down the Divine Muse". There are numerous examples of this in the Irish literary canon, and in the twentieth century literary world alone, the lives and works of Scott Fitzgerald, William Faulkner, Dylan Thomas, and Jean Rhys exemplify this. Others engaged in creative work, including actors, composers, and singers, use alcohol for its role-deepening and performance-easing properties. The second dimension of this "divine encountering experience" is also reliably invoked by its consumption, the God of social communion. Alcohol plays a fundamental role in hospitality, especially in Ireland but in many other communities too. It can engender conviviality and social intercourse, the proclivity to sing, dance and emote not least among its powers. Alcohol is used to foster agreements and contracts, and can also facilitate the forging of interpersonal and social bonds of immense and enduring significance. The number of deals done, bargains struck and marriages and trysts that owe a debt to it are beyond counting (notwithstanding the number undone in the equation!).

Another social necessity, intimacy, is documented as a difficulty, particularly but not exclusively for young Irish males. Could it be this that makes men so enjoy it — the gift of unguarded (if boozy) moments of mutual acceptability? The central psychic importance of intimacy is undoubted. And, having achieved it, experience of its loss, worsened too by alcohol, is the most common antecedent found in studies of suicides in Ireland and elsewhere (Bedford, 2001).

At least temporarily through alcohol, we can relate, belong and dissolve some of our differences. In having these capacities it mediates, however imperfectly, experience of the transpersonal domain. With it, the possibility of momentary transcendence and reconnection to cosmic and social unity for isolate man is renewed. By the capacity of alcohol to permit glimpses of the creative and communal aspects of the "divine", it achieves enormous cultural, even sacramental importance. This reflects the ancient "spiritual" utility of alcohol, an intoxicant that can powerfully convey us to this remote plane of experience, a point echoed and reinforced by a common linguistic root — "spiritus".

However, in addition to its association with the divine, alcohol is used sometimes to connect with our darker forces. In wartime, for instance, alcohol is used to evoke primitive destructive forces and feelings against the enemy and then unleash behaviour commensurate with these. Criminals, delinquents, football hooligans and rioters, to mention some examples, commonly use alcohol toward their ends.

In this "demonic" aspect (as the ballad goes "whiskey you're the devil . . ."), alcohol allows one not only to tap into important forces of destruction and negation but also hate and social violence. In having these aspects, alcohol mediates, also imperfectly, the arch-personal domain and with it the possibility of individual exaltation, the triumphal isolate denial of the cosmic and social order or status quo. The parallel social (or anti-social in fact) dimension is equally important if somewhat hidden. Enduring and powerful social conjunction is achieved or preserved by shared drunken taboo violations, typically but not always with socially dysfunctional elements of the community. The thrill of the rampage, the freedom from constraint, the settling of scores are enacted and fêted every weekend. The mechanisms by which such behaviour and sentiments are tolerated are psychologically simple; individual rationalisation and collective dilution of guilt through group dynamics facilitates the process effectively.

Psychological Hazards of Alcohol

Alcohol then can introduce us, relatively on demand, to remote and often hazardously accessible mental states that we desire. Perhaps we even *need* to access these, especially when the demands of conscious living overwhelm our coping repertoire, be it personal or cultural. This point is important to my thesis and will be returned to later.

These deeper experiences during intoxication are a form of encounter with our archetypal heroic and anti-heroic selves. By the same token, alcohol can also clearly drop us into these states unprepared, precipitously amplifying our dominant vulnerability with often catastrophic but no less predictable results. Furthermore, while it is clear we accept (and at times, even expect) a loss of control when in pursuit of these states, the lack of control is even greater than we allow for. It is also never mastered, despite experience.

We seek encounter with the heroic senses of power, skill, strength, success, freedom, wealth and sexual attractiveness or prowess. Acting from a newly valued self can lead to situations we might not otherwise have the confidence to seek out and from which we profit. The timid are thus emboldened, and sometimes but not always, rewarded — "he who dares . . ."?

However, those already confident can, in turn, become monstrous; alcohol inflating and aggrandising pre-existing feelings of self-satisfaction. The dinner party boor and the lager lout are one and the same. This enhanced confidence also leads to increasingly poor judgement. Sustained grandiose feelings and the illusion of immunity from the consequences of our actions are common, drunk driving and reckless gambling being only two examples.

Alcohol can also exaggerate and coarsen pre-existing anti-heroic self-loathing. Many alcoholics daily return to and confirm their sense of this. The anti-heroic realities of impotence, uselessness, weakness, failure, recklessness, impoverishment, sexual guilt and rejection, in equal measures, are the wellspring and end point of the alcoholic. The book and movie *Leaving Las Vegas* illustrates this theme exceptionally well. Worse perhaps, alcohol also catapults the unwary to this experience of the anti-heroic. In this respect it is a singularly powerful agent. One becomes irreversibly reduced overnight. Cumulatively, or less often precipitously, this experience of self-loathing leads, in some, to initiate depression and suicide.

Lastly, but importantly, one further aspect of the problem with alcohol intoxication is its capacity to deliver results not predicted by our intentions. While we seek experience or escape from the heroic or anti-heroic, we never know for certain when we take a drink which experience will transpire, and how, contrary to our plan this might (apparently uncharacteristically) affect our behaviour. Importantly, this effect is not dose-dependent in a simple linear plot. Four drinks won't have the same result on any two similar occasions, and the "one" extra can change the direction of the behaviour quite suddenly, unexpectedly and usually for the worse.

This capacity, to turn a good night bad in an instant, may explain some of the accounts of unexplained suicides, typically where the person seemed to all in robust and good spirits without any reason for suicide, the only apparent difference being a few drinks more than usual. This phenomenon has a likely partial basis in a lethal coincidence of biological (genetic) risk factors that engender unique vulnerability; benign, inconsequential and unknown until the night in question. These factors will be touched on later.

In trying then to fully understand why we are so enduringly fond of it, despite its risks, I finally must allow what I regard the pivotal but most oblique cultural function of alcohol. It serves not just to introduce us to our "divine" as well as our "shadow" or dark sides, but paradoxically to force us to return to and gain respect and mastery over our human limitations, despite having introduced us to these wondrous creative and destructive potentialities. Because it mainly only reveals the more arrogant and dismal aspects of our psychic range, we are increasingly forced to face the personal obligation for restraint and control. Part of the bargain is that we have to learn how to "hold our drink", usually by bitter and typically repeated experience. Information and warnings are signposts, but no substitute for the hard personal schoolroom of reverence and regret. This is perhaps why alcohol accompanies so many of our rites of passage.

The deeper understandings of our self-actualisation are withheld until we have learned this. It is in this respect that alcohol (and other intoxicants) instruct, for if we can practise restraint and come to respect our unconscious capacities, our education has begun — the reliance on alcohol to actualise our aspirations can be set aside, and self-knowledge can unfold. If we don't learn this, and more often we do not, the consequences are obvious. For some, the 12 Steps of AA become the way. For others, and for many suicides, alcohol has the capacity to impact so lethally that this opportunity is never presented.

I suggest, in conclusion to this section, what we have lost in contemporary Ireland is cultural and psychological knowledge and respect for alcohol's uses and powers — a recognition of the need for guidance through these minefields. In most traditional societies, elders guide, shape and interpret the passage through initiation rituals, guard and regulate access to the sacramental intoxicant. However here in Ireland, we no longer bring our parents to the pub, the priests and until recently the alcohol industry have fallen silent on the dangers. Diageo have recently taken up the baton with their responsible drinking advertising campaign, but many regard this as a cynical ploy to avert greater regulation. Meanwhile, a whole generation has learned that alcohol excess is normal, and we reap or dread the bitter harvest. Can Government adopt the mantle of the elder guide? I believe it can and should, and will return to this at the end.

Regulatory Forces and Influences

Next, I will outline the importance of social regulatory forces that shape the nature of our exposure to alcohol. The relevance of the *context* in which alcohol is consumed is highly significant. The outcome of ingestion of alcohol to a considerable extent depends on the context in which it occurs. The settings for consumption may be intimate or anonymous, collective or individual, celebratory or dolorous. Drinking alone, and indeed most hangovers, are known especially to lead to introspection, anomie and gloom. A social drinking session may be to rejoice or console, to seek courage or deflect from its want, to meet one's neighbour or destroy your enemy. Whether alcohol is consumed in a multi-generational or uni-generational ensemble, whether or not there are family or other communal influences, is also important in the experience and behavioural outcome. These conditions significantly determine how we behave. Most importantly, however, is the point that these conditions have changed remarkably in Irish society in only a generation, as have the resultant, negative behavioural outcomes.

There are also statutorily defined regulatory influences, setting age, time, place and historic gender limits on access to alcohol. Licensing and point-of-sale controls not only regulate the actual amount, but also the social context in which alcohol is to be consumed. The traditional bar was often a small, proprietor-run establishment, in your own neighbourhood, where control and regulation were a necessary and personally mediated part of the service. In order for public houses to remain licensed, they have to run their premises in a way that contains the risks and adverse consequences. This persists, but enforcement can appear arbitrary at best. In recent times, the regulatory environment itself has changed toward liberalisation, especially in licensing hours and pub character. These changes to regulatory forces are clearly linked to cultural outcomes, but it is hard to be certain whether culture or regulation is the prime mover for liberalisation. What is clear is that to re-assert control and induce cultural change, legal regulation at least has some influence and is crucial, but in itself is insufficient.

Historical Influences on, and Interpretations of, Consumption Behaviour in Ireland

Before I examine the present alcohol consumption culture I will consider historical descriptions and our international reputation for drunkenness. Regardless of the basis for this reputation, I suggest that we might begin from the premise that it is deserved and is a perspective we have to acknowledge. Some writers support the view that the origins of this image lay in reports of nineteenth century Irish emigrants to American and British cities. Dislocation, poverty, alienation, negative stereotyping and racism, a sense of failure — experiences of many migrant groups — may well have fuelled the escapism offered by alcohol. Additional explanations for alcohol excess in the Irish cite the response to colonialism, both in the form of British political oppression and control, and Roman clericalist dominance. True or not, the psychological significance is clear. Particularly for Ireland, or at least its peasant classes, the experience and expression of liberty became inextricably linked to alcohol use and misuse.

Historical circumstances offer some additional clues. Descriptions of Irish drunkenness are frequently dismissed as deliberate colonialist misrepresentations and part of a campaign to outlaw poitín. Under British and later Irish laws, the indigenous profitable cottage industry of poitín manufacture that was available to peasantry and beyond the reach of revenue was outlawed. The clergy, scandalised by its socially outlandish consequences, were zealous partners in its suppression.

Economic hopelessness and all its effects, the Famine and emigration, political and cultural oppression, all the woes of colonial reality were taken, seemingly legitimately, for consolation and cheer to the public house. As beer, stout, whiskey and cider manufacture became technologically sophisticated, it became centralised, and subsequently monopolised, by anglophile (and often protestant) family concerns. This paved the way for later branding and mass marketing. The export of alcohol became fundamental to the national economy. The revenue stream to government, colonial or native, was indispensable. Shop keeping and hence pub ownership (one of the few avenues of economic self-improvement available to the native landless who were precluded from the professions and better jobs) became a colluding and willing partner in the alcohol industry. A yard of bar counter was as profitable as many acres of land — hence the profusion of licences to sell it — and a legacy of so many places to buy it.

Of course, there are few alternatives anyway; the old adage that there is nothing to do in Ireland except go to the pub is to a large extent true, especially when you consider the low level of investment in community alternatives. Similarly, the ubiquitous presence of alcohol sale at sporting events and other clubs effectively means that we are surrounded on all sides anyway. This is not an accident of history. In Elizabeth Malcolm's paper, "The rise of the pub in Irish popular culture" (Malcolm, 1999), the reasons why public houses became so important and numerous in Ireland with the growth of towns are set out. Licensing was used by colonial governmental and clerical elements to control what were perceived as being revolutionary and permissive influences, sexual and political intrigue being especially subversive to the social order. Once licensing yielded the extent of revenue that it did, the then colonial and subsequently national government effectively became the sponsors of this system of drink purveyance. The pub became an effective agency and venue of social control. A further effect was the weakening of cultural antecedents of pre-pub Ireland. In particular, this had a destructive impact on indigenous cultural domains of sport, music and other forms of social encounter which underpinned Irish agrarian society of that time. The residual remnants of old culture were then re-enacted in the principal public space, the public bar, even up to the present. Irish culture and Irish social encounter became unwitting but enduring bedfellows of commercialised alcohol sale.

Whether this argument of colonial reaction is in fact part myth or part truth, it obscures a still deeper point. Our thinking has become colonised with our own self-justifying exculpatory mythology — it's just not our fault we drink so much. It is obvious, however, that alcohol, rather than being regarded as an act or agent of our liberation from these colonial forces and circumstances, is instead an instrument of our entrapment. It serves in denying us the opportunity and possibility of truly indigenous liberating and maturing alternatives, which remain forever adolescent instead. Then again, lack of a robust capacity for analytical self-criticism is supposedly yet another colonial legacy. But it is a persistent theme in commentary on our alcohol problem. The Celtic Tiger, European Union, modernism, globalisation and any other exogenous influence one cares to mention are listed as the corrupting enemy. No doubt these are important factors, but they should not blind us from our own complicity in incorporating them as pretexts to have yet another drink.

Increases in Alcohol Consumption in Recent Times in Ireland

Many reliable studies clearly document the pattern of increased alcohol consumption in Ireland. The interim report of the Strategic Task Force on Alcohol indicates the overall per capita consumption in Ireland for the year 2000 was 14.2 litres per person, and indicates in the ten preceding years that there was a 41 per cent increase in per capita consumption. There has been a 50 per cent increase in spirits and 100 per cent increase in the consumption of cider. In contrast, nine other European member states showed a decrease in alcohol consumption in the same period, while just three other countries showed any increase (and ones which were modest by comparison).

It is not alone those with high income who have increased consumption; all strata are involved. The European School Survey project in alcohol and other drugs indicates that Ireland is top of the league of underage drinkers with three-quarters of 15- and 16-year-olds drinking alcohol at least once a month, and one-third of them admitting to binge drinking on three or more occasions a month. The explosion in feral behaviour is evident everywhere. The National Lifestyle Survey of 1999 indicates that 18-24 and 25-34-year-old age groups drank less often than their older peers but were more likely to engage in high-risk drinking when they did. Compared to other age groups, much higher rates of over-65's drink five or more days a week (for example, 26.3 per cent of the older men and 33.0 per cent of the older women are drinking this frequently, compared with 4.9 per cent of the males aged 18-24 and 4.2 per cent of the women in the younger age group). While the level of high-risk drinking per session decreases compared with younger people, it is still 9.1 per cent among older men, and 11.1 per cent among older women.

The cost of alcohol abuse in Ireland is estimated by the European Comparative Alcohol Study at €2.4 billion annually, approximately 1.7 per cent of the gross domestic product, a figure that doesn't include costs such as health care, road accidents, alcohol-related crime and lost productivity.

Changes in Drinking Behaviour and Interactions with Culture in Ireland

How has this increase been brought about? There have been massive transformations in the cultural contexts and the regulatory environment of alcohol in the last several years in Ireland. These changes are testimony to the marketing ingenuity and indeed profitability of the licensed trade in Ireland. Vintners' interests have had a virtually free hand, our economic secret weapon, for the paranoiac, our own version of the "military-industrial complex". Government is *de facto* beholden through revenue, scarce through the lean times of the 1970s and 1980s. It leads however to questions concerning the infiltration, indeed creation, of aspects of Irish culture by the alcohol industry.

What is the role of advertising and marketing? The impact of advertising on consumption is undeniable, except of course by the drinks industry mysteriously given to fund it. Research here (Dring and Hope, 2001) shows alcohol ads have strong attraction: they reinforce beliefs; portray social, sexual and professional success linked to drinking; portray alcohol use as safe and risk-free; widen knowledge of alcohol use; and target young people despite protestations to the contrary. The younger age group, 12-14-year-olds, perceived that alcohol advertising says that alcohol helps them have fun, make friends and become popular, and that those who don't drink are missing out. The 15-17-year-old group believes the message that social success and a good time result from alcohol use. Alcohol advertising has skilfully stitched alcohol consumption to gender role anxieties as well, such that to be a "real man" or a "real woman" now involves heavy and public excess alcohol consumption. However, what is forgotten is that the female or adolescent body can only metabolise alcohol at half the rate as the adult male, and is significantly more susceptible to toxic consequences.

Relentless promotion of alcohol, as we experience at present, builds on historical stereotypes of our own image of a heavy drinking culture. This is despite undisputed high rates of absenteeism and a relatively low alcohol consumption rate internationally up to recently. This self-image of a heavy-drinking people with high tolerance for drunkenness has been the perfect cover for equally heavy promotion. Our misguided tolerance for excessive drinking opened the door for these initiatives and now the full extent of our drinking problem appears to come as a surprise. Our reputation is fast being revived that, if nothing else, we are world champion drunks.

The encroachment has not been on the population already drinking but instead relies on the creation of a new market. It has targeted the recruitment of new and freshly affluent segments — youths and females. This is comparable to the efforts of the tobacco industry in previous times, and has been highly effective. It has also been hugely successful and profitable. Unlike the wine industry in European markets, the extensive consolidation of beer and spirit manufacture in Ireland and internationally over the last 25 years lends itself to brand creation, promotion, loyalty and niche appeal. You can design, create and market a drink that will exactly fit a new market segment. Meanwhile, existing customers are rewarded with messages of nostalgia, pride and tradition. "Drinking for Ireland" is construed as part of one's civic duty, one's personal contribution to develop the economy. Even advertisements themselves, Guinness being a prime example, have cachet, art status and are a source of national satisfaction.

It's like admiring the decor as the ship begins to sink.

What other changes? Bars themselves have made women and children welcome where they previously felt uncomfortable; food and entertainment are promoted, and improved environments (including beer gardens and play areas for children!) are important selling points. They also usefully disguise, deflect attention away from, and normalise the core activity. The degree to which alcohol has insidiously infiltrated our ritual and ceremonial occasions is such that now we cannot even imagine many occasions without, not only the presence, but the dominating influence of alcohol.

Public binge drinking exploded during the last 25 years, associated largely with community and tourist festivals. Many of these are culturally shallow, sham occasions created by commercial interests with spurious links to history and location. The increase in the number of exemptions which allow for "extensions" of opening hours essential to their creation was *nine-fold* for the years 1967 to 1994. These were all judicially sanctioned. This change in judicial attitude and practice is as inexcusable as it is difficult to understand. However the same judiciary were still obligingly available at the next court sitting to prosecute the drunken casualties, in ever-increasing numbers, dispensing varieties of mercy or admonition with all the inconsistencies that refract our own peculiar national social mores on drunkenness.

Vintners' interests drove this phenomenon under the guise of tourism and cultural patronage, assisted by a poor public or political appetite to establish, or even seek, an alternative source of income. Sponsorship has become the essential ingredient to organising any community event. In addition, there have been very aggressive marketing programmes, skilfully woven into and targeting youth culture, with "Happy Hours", "All You Can Drink" promotions and several other events designed to maximise consumption. Such events stage-manage mass drunkenness at discounted prices attractive to youths, often with corporate, legal and communal endorsement.

Festivals and their real side-show became synonymous with tourism and have been effectively and lucratively incorporated into our own brand of national identity. Tourist advertisements for Ireland almost always include reference to alcohol and pubs as part of the campaign. The other main outlet for increased sales has been through growth in the number of restaurants with full licences, ostensibly for tourists but well adapted for natives through the "chicken and chips routine". Policing the licensing laws is unpopular, tied up with colonial "peeler" folk memories, and set at a level well above the statutes.

In addition to changing our rural and traditional identity, alcohol is now associated with "urban renewal". Dublin, like Newcastle, Reykjavik, Copenhagen and Ibiza, has fused economic reversal of inner city dereliction and a tourist industry with the number of bars and drinking clubs it offers to visitors and residents. Large intermediary managed super-pubs, catering to mainly anonymous and often exclusively younger customers, have developed, with drinking hours extending into the early morning and "Happy Hours" (when drinks, usually spirits, were made available for sale at reduced prices), presaging the "Misery Hours" of 2.00–4.00 a.m.

In 2000 alone there were almost 15,000 reported cases of intoxication in a public place and a similar number of cases of abusive or insulting behaviour. In an attempt to stem the huge growth of these offences the Irish Government updated the existing legislation, the Intoxicating Liquor Act, in 2000. They believed that by extending opening hours and liberalising the drinking regime people would respond by moderating their alcohol consumption — a dangerous delusion. An act of the Oireachtas alone will not make us behave like moderate southern Europeans. The situation then worsened, with alcohol consumption increasing further, and yet more incidences of violent behaviour.

Dublin city centre, like all the other smaller market towns swept along on the coat tails of urban renewal schemes, has been colonised at night by young people, packing these theme bars and pubs to bursting point. These licences were granted to the renewal schemes to entice and reassure the residents they would have something to do in the evening. This created not cafe culture but a late-night wasteland of drunkenness and violence, while the misled and stranded residents stay at home appalled and terrified in equal measure, awaiting the morning detritus of vomit, blood and broken glass. Early in 2003 laws were passed restricting "Happy Hours" and other discounting schemes, and a much tougher approach was promised to premises with recurring problems of violence and anti-social behaviour. Locking the stable door . . . ?

The off licence trade has also changed beyond all recognition, from the shameful hatch in the wall to brightly lit temples of temptation, selling glamorous portable alcohols, luxury ice cream, tantalising snack foods, tobaccos and other impulse merchandise! Others use wine clubs that deliver by post. This facilitates the normalisation of convenience and impulsive buying of alcohol for deregulated, and sometimes de-contextualised, consumption. Unregulated illegal sale, often to minors, is also a major problem — proxy buying by adults; illegal van sales in housing estates; drinks delivery services (similar to pizza); sales of smuggled alcohol by paramilitary interests; not to mention the perennials, shebeens, poitín and home brewing, each finding a place.

Sports clubs, golf, rugby and GAA also took on new licences and often sell at keen prices, not to mention hosting boozy weekend fundraising events. Sporting bodies in Ireland commonly use bars and hotels to present prizes and awards. The drinks company Diageo spends €40 million per annum on Irish advertising, with examples of sponsored events including the Carlsberg West Coast Challenge, Guinness Clarenbridge Oyster Festival, Galway Races, Coors Light European Body Board Cup, Heineken European Cup, and the Wittness two-day Music Festival, leaving few significant events which one can cite that don't have a branded alcohol product as part of its name.

Since 1995, Guinness has sponsored the All Ireland Hurling Championship on an ongoing contractual basis. The multimillion euro investment in the Hurling Championship and the fusion of these two national icons has been a major advertising and marketing coup. Since the deal, there has been substantial progress in attendance at matches with participation having doubled and a four-fold increase in matches shown on live television. Rugby has the Heineken Cup. However it is a Faustian compact, in that the sport has so prospered by this relationship it is now being manipulated by this level of sponsorship. It is then held to ransom, and effectively loses control of its own activity. All this without even mention of the messages, associations and consequences it creates.

Lastly, the growth in alcohol consumption paralleled the Irish version of the international movements of sexual and cultural liberation, the demise of "Old Ireland" and all its institutional pillars, Irish economic development, the sports movement, youth culture and laterally the renaissance of Irish cultural pride and achievement. In many senses, then, alcohol can claim extensive credit for lubricating the process of the tortuous and crazy experience of creating modern Ireland. It has become fused with people's biographical and sentimental journey through it. Having discovered ourselves and invented a modern culture with alcohol as our handmaiden, somewhere the personal and societal risk and costs of drunkenness were overlooked.

The extent to which sport and other domains of culture have been sold out to alcohol marketers begs an important question: whether alcohol is part of our culture, or whether our culture is part of the alcohol industry? This is the central point to my thesis. I suggest we have taken our eye off the cultural prize in our rush for economic development. We undervalue and underestimate the influence possible by enlightened government and leadership. There is no national state agency or ministry (unlike France, for example) truly directing or supporting cultural activity, especially popular and youth culture, and in its absence we entrust it to the safe hands of our largest but undeclared semi-state body, the drinks industry. Without being melodramatic, if not addressed, it can be construed as a form of cultural self-harm or even cultural suicide and is no less destructive. Having reclaimed a viable economy we must reclaim a viable society.

Cultural Disorientation and Alcohol Consumption

Ireland is presently the most globalised country in the world. The apparent willingness to tolerate this rapid rate of change, an orientation to European and American forces and a marked cultural permeability, partly explain our economic and social transformation. It has the effect, however, of disorienting us somewhat from our traditional collective unconscious. Our spiritual, familial, communal and historico-mythic unconscious has been supplanted by an unstable and uncertain culture of hedonism and individualism, living in the here and now, bordering at times on the reckless. The problem is that the traditional collective unconscious, which is the reservoir of our cultural identity and values, and what we need most when in this disoriented state, has been thrown into confusion, and sometimes disrepute, as part of our experience of globalisation.

Without wishing to excuse our drinking, it seems in order to cope with this disengagement, strategies to reconnect with our unconscious reservoirs are utilised for better or worse — buying goods and buying a good "old" time in an attempt to recover our most precious asset, innocence. Young people are most susceptible. This is well understood by the advertising industry, fostering consumerism by seeking out and attaching values to products that answer our cultural yearnings. Any prominent alcohol marketing campaign in Ireland in recent times, from the Budweiser frog, the Guinness "Giant" and "Believe" campaigns, Bulmer's "cider tradition", the Smithwicks' "Cheers" bar to mention only a few, exemplify this and its efficacy. However, in the case of alcohol, the product is not a soft drink or clothing, but a highly psychoactive substance, with a large propensity for addiction and with significant associated health problems, especially suicide.

Such is our uncertainty but also our majestic overconfidence that we are maximally impressionable to receive messages about who we are. However those who are telling us are often just selling to us. Hence the need for strict measures to reduce promotion and consumption, especially at times of greatest cultural change — exactly the opposite to what has happened here.

Correlations between Alcohol Consumption and Suicide Rates in Ireland

It is quite apparent from Central Statistics Office (CSO) figures that the most pronounced increase in Ireland's suicide rate in the last 15 years has been in the young male age group with an important link between alcohol consumption and suicide also evident. Figure 4.1, taken from work in press,[1] shows the relationship between suicide rates in men aged between 15 and 45 divided into three decade spans plotted against beer and wine and cider consumption taken together for the years 1988-2000. It is quickly evident the fluctuations in beer consumption closely track the fluctuations in suicide rates for men in these age spans.

---

[1] I would like to acknowledge my collaborators Paul Corcoran and Prof. Ivan Perry of the National Suicide Research Foundation, kindly supported by a research grant from the National Suicide Review Group.

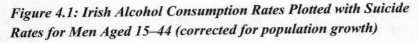

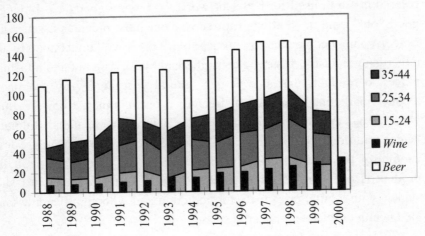

Figure 4.1: Irish Alcohol Consumption Rates Plotted with Suicide Rates for Men Aged 15–44 (corrected for population growth)

There is prior evidence from the scientific literature of co-variation of suicide rates and alcohol consumption from several studies. In several countries there are studies indicating the correlation between suicide rates and population alcohol consumption (Ramstedt, 2001). One Norwegian study (Rossow, 1995) indicated that this relationship was significant for women; a study also backed up by more recent evidence reported from the UK indicating that an increased suicide rate in young women is related to increases in alcohol consumption (McVeigh and Osman, 2002). A Finnish study (Makela, 1996) found, however, that the relationship was stronger for men.

As part of our study, alcohol consumption figures and suicide frequency figures from the Central Statistics Office were subject to differencing. This allows correlations of year-to-year differences, rather than year-on-year difference, in alcohol consumption and suicide figures. This corrects for autocorrelation in time series data. The suicide rate, rather than the raw figures, were correlated with the alcohol consumption level for beer, spirits, and wine and cider together for men and women in standardised age groupings.

Results from this study indicate that the correlation between alcohol consumption and population suicide rate did not reach statistical significance. However, there were significant correlations in the 25-34 and

45-54 age groups for wine and cider consumption for men, and also 15-24, 45-54 age brackets for beer consumption. For women, the only positive correlation was found for wine and cider consumption in the 10-15-year-old age group.

These are the first such correlations for Irish consumption figures and are broadly in keeping with internationally reported links. They demonstrate and emphasise the significant relationship between beer consumption and male suicide, in addition to wine and cider consumption taken together for men, and for the very young female group. Correlation is *not* causation, but there are extensive corroborating lines of evidence documenting the link between alcohol and suicide, some of which are outlined below, and this evidence remains key in explaining the increase in suicides in Irish men.

Obtaining consumption figures for wine, cider and alcopops separately is difficult due to the way in which these figures are recorded by the CSO. However, the Department of Revenue provided consumption details for these products as set out in Table 4.1.

Alcopops were only introduced and consumed in volume from 1995 onwards — an insufficient time for reliable correlations to emerge. However the findings are certainly worrying, given the massive increase in alcopop and cider consumption in Ireland over the period, and the fact that these products are extensively consumed and marketed to younger age groups.

Table 4.1: Alcohol Consumption (in litres of pure alcohol)

	Alcopops	Wine	Cider
1996	139,451	3,481,465	1,903,410
1997	191,811	3,785,997	2,174,700
1998	150,860	4,392864	2,481,721
1999	179,013	4,823,386	2,896,137
2000	523,762	5,538,067	3,355,378
2001	412,451	6,224,091	3,719,842
2002	591,998	6,939,087	3,336,177

With thanks to Michael McDonnell, Excise Statistics Unit, Revenue Commissioners, Ireland.

Their role in the rise in female youth suicide in Ireland is speculative and, given the low overall numbers, will be difficult to prove. There is less doubt about their role in youth female violence, sexual misadventure and rape victimisation, so a link to suicide will be unsurprising.

How Alcohol is Implicated in Suicide

It was Karl Meninger who made the observation between addictions as forms of suicidal behaviour, but there is also extensive evidence linking alcohol's effects on the brain to suicide. In the short term, alcohol increases impulsivity and reduces inhibition, increases aggression and may distort behaviour. It can induce emotional and perceptual distortion, change one's cognitive set, and exacerbate lowered mood. These acute effects of alcohol are a significant factor in facilitating suicidal acts.

We understand that alcohol consumption specifically occurring prior to a suicide attempt is a more important risk factor than the habitual alcohol consumption pattern of the individual (Borges et al., 1996). The clustering of suicides at weekends suggests that besides the established risk factors for suicide among alcohol misusers, the act of using alcohol per se further contributes to the suicidal act (Pirkola et al., 1997). It was found in one US study that 35.8 per cent of cases had a positive blood alcohol reading (Hayward et al., 1992) and Irish figures may be higher. Bedford, in his Irish study (Bedford, 2001), reports the high level of alcohol problems, with a third of males in the sample having a known history of alcohol abuse.

Quoting from the American Medical Association 2003 "Statement on the harmful consequences of alcohol use in the brains of children, adolescents and college students", it is clear that alcohol consumption by younger age groups is not merely a transitional or circumscribed problem, it puts them at much greater risk of subsequently developing adult alcohol-use disorders. Adolescents need only drink half as much as adults to experience the same negative effects as older counterparts, and there is significant evidence of damage to brain regions (including the hippocampus and the prefrontal area) as a result. These regions are important in learning and memory, and when impaired lead to the appearance of neurocognitive deficits which directly and negatively impact study habits and erode the development of transitional skills needed for successful progression to adulthood. These essential developmental skills are likely important in protecting against suicide in young people.

There is also a significant body of literature on the relationship between alcohol and its effects on mood, but more particularly there are now considerable links between serotonin abnormalities, associated with suicide, and alcohol use. There are acute effects of alcohol on promoting serotonergic neurotransmission, causing euphoria, and importantly the reverse effects on mood during alcohol withdrawal. Persistent alcohol abuse also reflects, among other things, a requirement for euphoria, suggested from both primate and human studies. In adult nonhuman primates who underwent early developmental stress, variables indicating a low serotonin turnover rate were associated with behavior patterns similar to those predisposing to early-onset alcoholism among humans by findings of lower serotonin, present from early development in predisposed individuals (Higley and Bennet, 1999). A functional variant(s) in or close to the TPH gene involved in serotonin may predispose individuals to suicidality (Nielsen et al., 1998). Excess alcohol intake is also related to impulsive aggression, partially mediated by negative mood states as part of a serotonin derangement, including serotonin transporter availability (Heinz et al., 1998, 2001).

The importance of this emerging neuroscientific evidence is that it challenges the notion that alcohol misuse is not directly linked to suicide, that the association is spurious, linked instead to more complex, more socio-cultural variables. Crucially, in contrast, together with the other findings, it points to the central mediating role of alcohol in many suicides. Alcohol misuse is not just a symptom of lethal social malaise. It, in itself, has lethal potential. It is a potent destabiliser of mood and behaviour. Many of the social and individual precursors to suicide are either potentiated or precipitated by it. Culture here concords with biology in fact, despite attempts to set them at odds. Reducing alcohol consumption won't cure all Ireland's social ills, but it may lead to a lower suicide rate.

Cultural and Other Responses to Reduce Alcohol Excess and Suicide Rates

What then are possible responses to this challenge? The greater control of sales and merchandising, in conjunction with regulation and enforcement, are key strategies — policing the edges of supply and demand. The National Alcohol Policy indicates the two most effective measures are limiting availability and increasing cost. There is strong evidence that such policies have a positive impact. However, public support, enforcement and long-term implementation of the policies are necessary for success. In Ireland, alcohol consumption is more sensitive to income increases than to price increases and, worryingly, is consequently likely to increase alongside and, if left unchecked, match the pace of economic growth. Pricing policies can encourage switching to forms of drinks with lower concentrations of alcohol, but the gradient must be steep. At present, it is not. Spirits are still better value for price-conscious youngsters, especially in off licences.

The Strategic Task Force on Alcohol recommendations emphasise the need to protect children and reduce pressure on adolescents through a number of measures. In 2001, the framework document for college alcohol policy represented a significant step forward in reducing alcohol marketing and promotion in colleges. But the problem is far too widespread and embedded to be tackled by legislation alone. Expecting the police to effect widespread social change, as is constantly cited as crucial, is, for me, like asking them to police the weather. We must build our own shelter. Alcohol education in schools, alcohol-free activities for young people, voluntary codes of bar practice, regulating the content of alcohol advertising, and putting warning labels on alcoholic beverage containers are politically popular measures but are of limited use. Unpopular but more effective measures are thus quietly parked. The benefits from such change will take a lot longer to see than the life of a government, shy of powerful lobbies and revenue loss. However, we *need* a long-term implementation plan of our alcohol strategy as a matter of utmost urgency.

Information, education and individual strategies can promote positive change in lifestyle habits through awareness raising, health promotion interventions and treatment services. Education from an early age is proposed as a solution, with a view to adopting a more mature, Mediterranean view of alcohol. This naive view overlooks the necessity for parents to stop "drinking like the Irish" and model a healthier approach and attitude towards alcohol, and an acceptance that even if behaviour patterns change, we, like our Mediterranean counterparts, will still face a higher rate of death as a result of cirrhosis. Wine consumption here is on top of, not instead of, what we already drink. Certainly enforcing advertising standards is important and increasingly complaints against alcohol advertisements have been successfully upheld, however there is no doubt that the availability of accessible and timely alcohol counselling services also needs to be improved.

In general, public health programmes address the conscious domain. However, I would suggest that perhaps a broader approach to the problem might prove fruitful. In particular, I think there are communal and cultural responses possible which tap a deeper level of our unconscious and release imaginative and creative solutions to this question. Perhaps first, we need a change of heart to enable us to confront our denial of the problem. The first step on the 12 Step AA Programme, which "admits powerlessness over alcohol and the unmanageability of our lives as a consequence", is perhaps a step we could take as a people and collectively as a nation, or at least be challenged to take. Finding a sector or figure sufficiently uncompromised to do so has been an additional difficulty.

Specifically, at the cultural level, we need to put alcohol in better proportion to our concepts of leisure, relaxation and pleasure. Perhaps we also need to confront the double-think which currently exists, and recognise that the alcohol industry, in promoting its seemingly benign and economically valuable interests, is in fact a government created monopoly purveying a sometimes dangerous, and potentially lethal, psychoactive drug with equivocal net benefit to the national purse. Then again, pigs might fly.

We could also change our notions about alcohol being the agent of our liberation and regard it instead as a cunning controller. Perhaps there is room for community leaders to speak out more, but when they do it can create a furore, a furore we are not willing to deal with. It was President McAleese who used the phrase that perhaps "we need to re-imagine an Ireland" in her remarks made in the United States in May 2003 (*Irish Times*, 2003). This is exactly apt and points to the need for a leap of imagination in forging our evolving cultural identity. This can be achieved through greater governmental involvement in the regulation and promotion of culture. At a policy level, culturally non-negotiable assets need to be recognised, valued and protected. The guardians of our most important cultural inheritance have to increase their awareness of their crucial role in protecting our cultural legacy from the infiltration and entrapment of alcohol marketing. We need to reduce and restrict alcohol sponsorship of cultural events. In particular, government funding of sporting and cultural activities should be contingent upon the *absence* of alcohol industry sponsorship. Instead of coming from health or moralistic perspectives on alcohol abuse alone, the positive promotion of leaders and role models from groups which champion temperate use can act as a positive step. The reduction of alcohol consumption could, instead of being a health objective, become part of *a national cultural project* which we might well do with anyway.

The challenge is to imagine and actualise an Irish society where alcohol has its place, not as the central aspect of culture, but merely one of the many ingredients that make up our identity. The challenge is also about actualising a less suicidal society, a society where self-fulfilment and self-creation have more romantic appeal and prospect of celebration than self-negation, self-destruction or self-indulgence.

References

Bedford, D. (2001) "Suicide in Ireland: A National Study". North Eastern Health Board Department of Public Health, Kells: Ireland.

Borges, G. and Rosovsky, H.. (1996.) "Suicide attempts and alcohol consumption in an emergency room sample". *J. Stud. Alcohol* 57 (5):543-548.

Brophy, J. (*in press*). "The Capture and Ransom of the Hound of Ulster", paper presented at the Annual Conference of the Irish Association of Suicidology 2003, Killarney, Ireland. www.ias.ie.

Dring, C. and Hope, A. (2001) "The Impact of Alcohol Advertising on Teenagers in Ireland", Health Promotion Unit, Department of Health and Children.

Hayward. L., Zubrick. S. R. and Silburn. S. (1992) "Blood alcohol levels in suicide cases". *J. Epidemiol. Community Health* 46 (3):256-260.

Health Promotion Unit, Department of Health and Children. Dublin, Ireland.

Heinz, A. et al. (2001) "Serotonergic Dysfunction, Negative Mood States, and Response to Alcohol" *Alcoholism: Clinical and Experimental Research* 25, No. 4.

Heinz, A., Higley, J.D., Gorey, J.G., Saunders, R.C., Jones, D.W., Hommer, D., Zajicek, K., Suomi, S.J., Lesch, K.P., Weinberger, D.R. and Linnoila, M. "In vivo association between alcohol intoxication, aggression, and serotonin trans-porter availability in nonhuman primates" (1998) *Am.J.Psychiatry* 155, 8, 1023.

Higley, J.D and Bennett, A.J. (1999) "Central Nervous System Serotonin and Personality as Variables contributing to Excessive Alcohol Consumption in Non-human Primates" *Alcohol and Alcoholism* Vol. 34, No. 3, pp. 402-418.

Makela, P. (1996) "Alcohol consumption and suicide mortality by age among Finnish men, 1950-1991". *Addiction*, 91, 101-112.

Malcolm, E. (1999) "The rise of the pub" from *Irish Popular Culture 1650-1850*, Dublin: Irish Academic Press.

McVeigh, T. and Osman, B. (2002) "Drinking is blamed as teen girl suicides soar", *The Observer*, September 29.

Nielsen, D.A., Virkkunen, M., Lappalainen, J., Eggert, M., Brown, G.L., Long, J.C., Goldman, D. and Linnoila., M. (1998) "A tryptophan hydroxylase gene marker for suicidality and alcoholism" *Arch Gen Psychiatry* 55(7):593-602.

Pirkola, S., Isometsa, E., Heikkinen, M., et al. (1997) "Employment status influ-ences the weekly patterns of suicide among alcohol misusers". *Alcohol Clin. Exp. Res.*, 21, 1704-1706.

Plant, M. (2001) *European School Survey Project on Alcohol and Other Drugs* (ESPAD).

Ramstedt, M. and Hope, A. (2002) "The Irish drinking culture — Drinking and drinking-related harm: A European comparison". Department of Health and Children Dublin, Ireland.

Ramstedt, M. (2001a) "Per capita alcohol consumption and liver cirrhosis mor-tality in 14 European countries", *Addiction*, 96, Supplement 1, S19-S34.

Ramstedt, M. (2001b) "Alcohol and suicide in 14 European countries". *Addic-tion*, 96 Suppl 1, S59-S75.

Ramstedt, M. (2002) "Alcohol consumption and the experience of adverse con-sequences — a comparison of six European countries", *Contemporary Drug Problems* 29:549-575.

Rossow, I. (1995) "Regional analyses of alcohol and suicide in Norway: some empirical considerations". *Suicide Life Threat.Behav.*, 25, 401-409.

Stockholm: Swedish Council for Information on Alcohol and Other Drugs (CAN).

Contextualising Consumption

Chapter 5

THE YOUTH OF IRELAND

Ian McShane
TNS mrbi, Dublin, Ireland

In September of 2003, *The Irish Times* and TNS mrbi published a series of three reports based on the findings of a comprehensive survey which covered all aspects of the life of a typical 15-24-year-old in Ireland today. This piece represents an edited version of the articles originally published in *The Irish Times*. The survey upon which the findings are based was conducted in-home over the August to September period 2003. In terms of subject matter, the interview ranged from general attitudes on the one hand to sexual activity and illicit drug-taking behaviour on the other. In order to protect the sensitivities of the younger adults being interviewed, as well as ensuring as honest a response as possible, the questions relating to the more personal topics were completed in private by the respondent by way of a self-completion form. Any queries the respondent may have had in relation to these questions were dealt with on the spot by the surveyer, although the majority of interviewees were happy to complete this form unaided, place it into a sealed envelope, and return it to the surveyer with their anonymity guaranteed.

The result is one of the most comprehensive social studies of the youth of Ireland in recent times, a constituency which according to the most recent Central Statistics Office data equates to 640,000 individuals. The first section of this report looked at this generation's attitudes towards, and usage of, tobacco, drugs and alcohol.

In terms of tobacco consumption, it is perhaps not surprising that four in ten 15-24-year-olds claim to smoke cigarettes, while the average age at which youngsters begin smoking is 14. A small majority (53 per cent) agreed with the ban on smoking in pubs and restaurants from March 2004, with a sizeable 43 per cent opposed to it.

Table 5.1 below sets down the proportion of 15-24-year-olds who drink alcohol nowadays, cross-analysed by the various age categories.

Table 5.1: Whether Drink Alcohol (%)

Base: All 15-24-year-olds	Total	15-17 yrs	18-19 yrs	20-22 yrs	23-24 yrs
Yes	80	60	87	91	83
No	20	40	11	9	17
No reply	—	—	2	—	—

It is clearly a fact of life that a majority of 15-17-year-olds drink alcohol nowadays, with a quarter of them allowed to do so at home. On average, young Irish people who drink alcohol start doing so at 16 years of age, a finding which is consistent across all areas of the country, and amongst those from all socio-economic backgrounds. It could be argued that this entry age to alcohol is not particularly low in itself, compared for example to continental Europe where many young adults drink alcohol with their meals as a matter of course. Indeed, in Ireland the debate in relation to alcohol consumption amongst young people tends to have centred on the types of drink consumed and the role of the alcohol industry in recruiting younger drinkers to their own brands. On the first point, it is true that a 15-17-year-old is more likely to prefer drinking an alcopop or cider than is a 23- or 24-year-old who is relatively more likely to opt for lager or even stout. Surely the question, though, is whether younger drinkers have been drawn into consuming alcohol per se by way of advertising and promotions for alcopop and cider brands, or whether they are likely to begin drinking as a rite of passage at 16 years of age regardless, and choose these types of drinks simply because they represent a more palatable alternative to beer and spirits.

The results of this survey suggest that teenage drinkers are actually consuming *less* alcohol per capita than are those in their early twenties — the real volume is being driven by lager, the consumption of which increases with age. Perhaps the emphasis therefore should be less on the route by which young people are introduced to alcohol, and more on the promotion of healthy and moderate consumption patterns as in other countries around the world. It is interesting to note for example that just under half of all 15-24-year-olds agree with the statement "I love the buzz of drinking". Coupled with the fact that drinkers in this age bracket consume a considerable eight drinks "on a good night out", a campaign focusing on the role of alcohol as a social lubricant as just one of many elements of a good night out might strike a chord.

In addition to alcohol and tobacco, respondents were asked which of a number of illicit drugs including cannabis, cocaine, ecstasy, heroin and speed they had ever tried, or indeed use regularly (see Table 5.2). In interpreting the responses to these questions, some findings from previous studies may prove useful. Historically, surveys of drug use in Ireland have tended to focus on adolescents and young adults in Dublin. For example, a study of teenage drug use in North Dublin conducted by the Royal College of Physicians in Ireland as long ago as 1996 indicated that lifetime use of the four most commonly used drugs stood at 60 per cent. This survey indicates that 59 per cent of 15-24-year-olds in the greater Dublin area have tried at least one of the five drugs listed. Research conducted by TNS mrbi for the Decode[*] consortium in 2000 found that of all 18-24-year-olds in Ireland, 41 per cent had ever tried an illicit drug. The *Irish Times*/TNS mrbi poll shows that 44 per cent of 15-24-year-olds nationwide have behaved similarly. While not directly comparable due to differing sample universes and data collection methods, all of these studies nevertheless show us that experimentation with drugs by younger individuals in Ireland has been widespread for quite some time now, and is likely to remain so for some time to come.

---

[*] Decode is a grouping of media and marketing practitioners which at the time of the 2000 research included Irish International, 98FM, TV3, TDI, *The Star* and Carlton Screen.

Table 5.2: Illicit Drug Usage (%)

Base: All 15-24-year-olds	Ever Tried	Regularly Use
Cannabis/marijuana/hash	39	11
Cocaine	9	1
E (ecstasy)	12	3
Heroin	3	—
Speed	10	1
Any of these illicit drugs	44	14

As to how to deal with this issue, it is key to note that there is a vast difference between the manner in which younger people view the "softer" drugs such as hash and cannabis, and "harder" drugs such as heroin. Indeed, focus group research amongst this population consistently suggests that a "continuum of acceptability" exists, ranging from hash or cannabis, which are seen by many to be no more harmful than alcohol, to ecstasy, which although widely available is recognised to have potentially catastrophic physical side-effects, to cocaine and heroin, which are very much at the outer extremities of acceptability.

It is for this reason that the vast majority of respondents who tell us they are regular users of drugs are in fact using cannabis/marijuana/hash, and have in the main rejected all others. If the predominantly male use of such soft drugs is to be reduced, their users will first need to be convinced that they are likely to be as harmful to them as is the alcohol which their parents consume so conspicuously.

Relationships and Sex

The next section of this report focuses on 15-24-year-olds' attitudes to sex and relationships, including their use of contraception as a barrier to pregnancy and/or sexually transmitted diseases.

With a view to setting the findings from this section into a sociological context, information was gathered at the outset of the interview in relation to the respondents' current domestic situation, insofar as this is one dynamic which is likely to influence the manner in which they conduct their own relationships. The first point to make in this regard is that over eight in ten of all 15-24-year-olds live at home with their parents, and are only beginning to move out in any numbers once they reach 23 or 24 years of age. We know from recently published Central Statistics Office data that this is very much part of a sociological trend, whereby the number of people in their late twenties and early thirties still living in the family home has burgeoned over the last ten years or so, not least because of the difficulties they are experiencing gaining a foothold on the property ladder.

Some commentators have posed the question as to what effect this is likely to have on the very nature of adult relationships in the future. Early evidence from this poll suggests that it may in fact have little or no effect, with younger dependents very much living their own lives when it comes to sexuality and relationships. Another point to note is that while one in six of this generation have parents who are either separated or divorced, the great majority of them live in the more "traditional" Irish home whereby both parents are still married.

As with the previous section's findings in relation to alcohol and drug use, the results concerning sexual activity seem to be broadly in line with academic studies conducted in Ireland over the last number of years. For example, MacHale and Newell conducted a survey of 15-18-year-olds at post-primary school in Galway in 1997 which indicated that 21 per cent had previous sexual experience, and that the average age at which they had first had sex was 15.5 years. A sub-analysis of the behaviour of 15-17-year-olds from this poll indicates that 25 per cent of them have had sex, and that the average age at which they first did so was 15.1 years. In overall terms, however, 18 seems to mark a significant turning point in the lives of today's youth in terms of sexual awakening, with seven in ten of all 18-19-year-olds having had sex at least once.

Table 5.3 below illustrates the proportion of young adults, cross-analysed by age sub-category, who have ever had sex.

Table 5.3: Ever Had Sex (%)

Base: All 15-24 year-olds	Total	15-17 yrs	18-19 yrs	20-22 yrs	23-24 yrs
Yes	62	25	68	78	85
No	37	74	31	21	14
Not stated	1	1	1	1	1

There is also evidence to suggest that any taboos which may have existed in the past in relation to sex and sexuality are fast disappearing. As mentioned, one of the survey's introductory questions identified that the vast majority of 15-24-year-olds are still living in their family home with their parents. As such, it can be assumed that the youth of today is subject to some extent to the moral codes of the parents whose home they share. It is interesting therefore to note that a majority of those who have had sex claim their parents are fully aware of the fact, a figure which peaks amongst female respondents. The implication is that the younger adult does not view his or her sexuality as something to be hidden from the older generation.

From a healthcare perspective, two key questions must relate to the degree to which this more sexually active younger generation is as a result more at risk from unwanted pregnancy and/or sexually transmitted diseases. At an overall level, results appear reasonably encouraging. Thus, while the number of partners those who are sexually active have had stands at seven by the time they reach 23 or 24 years of age, nine in ten of them claim that they usually use contraceptives, mainly as a barrier to both pregnancy and sexual diseases. Having said that, there are an estimated 40,000 young adults claiming to regularly engage in unprotected sex. Educationalists will presumably take note.

Finally, lest some should interpret these findings as a sign that fundamental family values are under threat in the future, it should be noted that the great majority of these young adults disagree with the statement "I feel that I will be married more than once in my life". Some of these are likely to have no intention of becoming married at all, but many clearly aspire to stability in their relationships as they grow older, just as their parents did.

Media Consumption and Social Issues

This final section provides an overview of this generation's views and experiences in relation to matters ranging from media consumption and diet, through to politics and religion.

Anyone involved in the media and marketing industry will be keenly aware that, while notoriously difficult to reach by conventional methods, the 15-24-year-old audience is nevertheless extremely media literate, and technologically savvy. The current poll, for example, tells us that over 90 per cent of this group own a mobile telephone, and the degree to which this generation communicates via texting, utilising what has in effect evolved into a distinct dialect of the English language, is by now well documented. In addition, almost two-thirds have access to the Internet, either at home, school/college or work, with the vast majority of these regularly using e-mail. They will also spend up to three hours each day watching TV.

Contrary to the common perception of a generation which has little or no interest in national or international affairs, a sizeable 85 per cent plus of this age group reads newspapers, with a small majority of these (equating to approximately 300,000 individuals) telling us they like to read about national and international news or politics. This is not to lose sight of the fact that sport is the key attraction of newspapers to the young Irish male, with celebrity news and entertainment the greatest draw for young females.

On a related point, one in eight of all 15-24-year-olds habitually view newspaper websites on-line, with one in seven regularly accessing Internet chat rooms, the latter behaviour more prevalent amongst the younger, and potentially more vulnerable, 15-19-year-old grouping. Regardless of the consequences of all of these findings for the media and marketing industry, they also of course have implications for educationalists, public health specialists and Government organisations which are constantly seeking to identify channels of communication by which they can effectively and credibly reach young people.

Having identified the quite significant number of younger adults who express an interest in national and international current affairs, it is worth referring to the responses elicited by a question which asked the interviewees to identify, on an unprompted basis, three people they most admire nowadays, and three people they least admire (Table 5.4). With regard to this generation's "heroes", a majority of them look to the type of people who have a direct influence on their lives on a day-to-day basis, including their parents (35 per cent), other family members (15 per cent) and friends and neighbours (26 per cent). Pop/rock stars (31 per cent) and sports stars (25 per cent) also elicit some admiration, with Bono/U2 and Roy Keane each mentioned by 8 per cent.

Table 5.4: Three People Most/Least Admired Nowadays: Main Replies (%) (unprompted)

Base: All Aged 15-24 Years	Most Admire	Least Admire
Parents	35	2
Other family member	15	2
Friends/neighbours	25	11
Roy Keane	8	2
David Beckham	4	4
Other sports people	18	10
Bono/U2	8	—
Eminem	3	—
Other pop/rock star	23	—
Mary McAleese	3	—
Nelson Mandella	4	—
George Bush	—	18
Bertie Ahern	—	15
Tony Blair	—	7
Ian Paisley	—	3
Charlie Haughey	—	2
Liam Lawlor	—	2
Charlie McCreevy	—	2

It is, however, particularly interesting to note that almost one in five of all Irish 15-24-year-olds name George Bush as one of the three people they least admire, on a purely unprompted basis. This compares with 7 per cent who mention both Tony Blair and Saddam Hussein in the same context. It is clear that the youth of Ireland is less than impressed with the current US administration's response to the events of 11 September 2001. Note that due to the fact that respondents were encouraged to name three people at this question, responses will add to more than 100 per cent.

Closer to home, the recent slide in Bertie Ahern's personal popularity also registers in the survey, with one in seven of our respondents spontaneously identifying the Taoiseach as someone they least admire nowadays. Incidentally, 17 per cent of those eligible to vote, and who tell us they are likely to do so in the 2004 local and European elections, single out the Taoiseach for criticism at this question.

There has been much debate of late in relation to the issue of healthy diet and weight control, and the related area of teenage eating disorders. With regard to healthy eating, almost half of these young adults (45 per cent) report that they do not have regular meal-times, a finding which is not particularly surprising, given the hectic lifestyle they lead. Of greater concern, however, is the fact that almost four in ten of them admit that they do not eat a healthy or balanced diet, a figure which is reasonably constant across the age groups, right up to those who are 23 and 24 years old.

Another figure which may set alarm bells ringing from a healthcare perspective is the extremely high percentage, 42 per cent, of young women who agree to the statement "I am always trying to lose weight". It seems unlikely that approaching half of all young females are overweight, which suggests there are many who are dieting so as to conform to a certain societal body-image. The downside to this dynamic is reflected in the fact that 56 per cent of all 15-24-year-old females know someone in their own age group who suffers from an eating disorder such as anorexia or bulimia.

And finally, what of the hopes and ambitions of this generation, the people who will in effect form the fabric of Irish society over the next ten to twenty years? At an overall level, seven in ten of them still tell us that they believe "Ireland is a good place for young people", for all its faults. As to what they feel those faults are (Table 5.5), the level of crime and street violence is a major concern, with over six in ten worried that Irish people are becoming more racist. Older respondents worry about the economy, with half of all young adults afraid they will never be able to afford a house or apartment in Ireland. And apart from family and friends, what are these young people likely to draw comfort from as they face into such an uncertain future? Those who profess to a belief in God are split 50/50 between those who participate in Mass and those who don't. There is broader consensus, however, on the importance of material comfort and financial security, with seven in ten of the up and coming generation agreeing that "money is very important to me".

Table 5.5: Agreement with Statements about Ireland (%)

Base: All Respondents 15-24 Years	Total	15-17 years	18-19 years	20-22 years	23-24 years
I am concerned regarding the level of crime and street violence	77	69	76	81	83
Ireland is a good place for young people	69	71	69	65	71
Criminal sentences are not long enough	68	62	65	74	73
Irish people are becoming more racist	62	57	63	63	64
I will never be able to afford a house/apartment in Ireland	50	49	53	52	46
I worry about the state of the economy	46	35	36	54	61

Chapter 6

BINGE DRINKING AND THE CONSUMPTION OF PLEASURE

Paula Mayock
Children's Research Centre, Trinity College Dublin

In common with other cultures, Irish culture is generally characterised by ambivalence towards alcohol, and ongoing public tolerance of alcohol-related problems has been interspersed with periods of heated public debate about the scale and broader societal impact of these problems. In what might appear, at least to its critics, to be a moral panic, the media have given extensive coverage in recent times to the changes which have taken place in patterns of levels of alcohol consumption in this country. The period between mid-2002 and mid-summer 2003 was one of unprecedented public attention — coupled with persistent and, at times, hostile debate — on the issue of drinking in Ireland (Butler, 2003). This coincided with the publication of the *Interim Report* of the Strategic Task-Force on Alcohol (2002), which was unambiguous in its presentation of a dramatic upward trend in rates of alcohol consumption in the general population. At the same time, both print and broadcast media devoted sustained negative attention to alcohol consumption and, in particular, to "binge" drinking, a style of alcohol consumption associated primarily with teenagers and young adults.[1] Indeed, the weight of nega-

---

[1] Alcohol use was the subject of literally scores of articles that appeared in the print media during this period. Some of the sensationalist headlines include: "Drunken binges

tive attention has fallen on young drinkers, not least because of some quite compelling evidence that alcohol consumption rates amongst youth have increased dramatically, particularly during the past decade. Current concerns about alcohol consumption amongst the young centre on heavy sessional or "binge" drinking and levels of reported (and apparent) drunkenness. However, despite the level of public attention to youth and alcohol, few attempts have been made to place youthful drinking patterns in the context of broader patterns of social life and living.

This chapter examines the phenomenon of "binge" drinking amongst the young in Ireland and offers a perspective on this contemporary drinking style that locates it in the context of wider social, economic and cultural changes. Divided into four sections, the chapter begins by briefly reviewing available research evidence pertaining to alcohol consumption in an Irish context, with a particular focus on young people. The following two sections broaden the focus with a discussion of youth lifestyles, consumer culture and the alcohol market. The aim here is to relate alcohol consumption to youth cultural forms, consumption patterns and changing economic circumstances and lifestyles. The final section draws on a recently-conducted study of drug and alcohol use amongst inner-city youth in an effort to illustrate the *meaning* of "binge" or "heavy sessional" drinking among young people within contemporary drinking scenes.[2]

---

fuel violence on streets (O'Riordan, 2002); "Young binge drinkers show signs of sclerosis" (O'Brien, 2003); "Some of them are drinking mixtures that would kill a horse" (Shanahan, 2003); "Young Irish biggest binge drinkers" (Cassidy, 2003); "Drowning in Drink" (Holmquist, 2003); "Survey shows increase in binge drinking" (Donnellan, 2003a); "The demon drink is a killer virus" (Brown, 2003); "High alcohol levels in women at assault unit" (Donnellan, 2003b).

[2] The term "binge drinking" is notoriously ambiguous and there is great inconsistency in how it is used and defined. Noting that researchers have been using the term "binge" or "binge drinking" to describe quite different phenomena, the *Journal of Studies on Alcohol* recently issued new guidelines to authors and has outlined a policy that requires the term "binge" to be used in a specific way in accepted manuscripts (see http://www.rci.rutgers.edu/~cas2/journal/Binge.html). This paper uses the term "binge" interchangeably with "heavy episodic drinking". No attempt is made to quantify a "binge"; rather the emphasis is on exploring a *style* of drinking characterised by the consumption of large amounts of alcohol during a single drinking occasion.

Overview of Drinking Trends amongst the Young

In the last decade, Ireland has seen many social changes that have undoubtedly influenced the nature of drinking. Against a backdrop of unprecedented economic growth and prosperity, Ireland also has had the highest increase in alcohol consumption among EU countries during the past decade. While trends in alcohol consumption per adult (that is, individuals over 15 years of age) over the past 40 years show a gradual increase up to the mid-1990s, there has been a dramatic rise in alcohol consumption since 1995. Between 1989 and 1999, alcohol consumption per capita in Ireland increased by 41 per cent (Strategic Task Force on Alcohol, 2002). This increase is highly significant in its own right but is even more striking in a European context, where there has been a downward turn in consumption rates in most countries during this same period. In 2000, the total alcohol consumption per adult was 14.2 litres of pure alcohol, compared to an EU average of 9.1 litres of pure alcohol per capita.

Ireland has traditionally had a significant number of total abstainers from alcohol, both in the general population (Cassidy, 1997) and among youth (O'Connor, 1978; Grube and Morgan, 1986). In view of the radical pace of social change in Ireland, one might expect a significant decline in the number of abstainers in the past 10-20 years and that this decline might, in turn, partly account for the apparent increase in the average amount consumed per person. However, a recent analysis of drinking habits in six European countries, including Ireland, found that the increase in per capita alcohol consumption in Ireland could not be explained by a decline in abstinence (Ramstedt and Hope, 2003). This study found that binge drinking was the norm among men, and that it occurs in about a third of women's drinking episodes, leading the authors to conclude that binge drinking is "strikingly common" in Ireland (Ramstedt and Hope, 2003).

We can now look to patterns and trends in alcohol consumption amongst the young using various data sources. The Health Behaviour in School-Aged Children (HBSC) survey (Friel et al., 1999) showed that over half of Ireland's young people begin experimenting with alcohol before the age of 12. By the time young people reach the age of 15 or 16, half of the girls and two-thirds of the boys are current drinkers (Hibell et al., 2000). The most recent *National Health and Lifestyle Survey*

(Kelleher, 2003) found practically no class effect in the numbers of children and young people reporting either lifetime or more recent alcohol consumption. Other striking changes are evident when the findings of this survey are compared to the 1998 equivalent (Friel et al., 1999). For example, while in 1998 there was a clear gender difference in reports of having been "really drunk", no such difference (31 per cent of boys and 30 per cent of girls) was found in the 2002 survey. In addition, the consumption of alcopops[3] among girls more than doubled from 3.1 per cent in 1998 to 8.1 per cent in 2002. In other words, the traditional association between alcohol consumption and male working class youth culture has fragmented; irrespective of gender, young people of all social classes are experimenting with alcohol at an early age and many are current or regular drinkers by their late teenage years.

In attempting to analyse and account for current drinking trends among the young, it is important to be clear that even one or two decades ago, post-primary school pupils reported high rates of lifetime drinking. For example, in 1984 a lifetime prevalence rate of 79.2 per cent was found for alcohol among 17-year-olds (Grube and Morgan, 1986); by 1992, this figure stood at 92.7 per cent for those aged 17 years and above (Morgan and Grube, 1994). Although these figures illustrate an increase in the number of young people reporting lifetime use of alcohol between 1984 and 1992, students' reported frequency of *being drunk* was far more noteworthy (Morgan and Grube, 1997). More significant, in other words, than the increase in rates of alcohol consumption is evidence pointing to a perceptible change in the *ways* in which young people are consuming alcohol, with drinking to intoxication a key feature of contemporary approaches to alcohol use amongst the young (Morgan, 2003). The results of two consecutive European School Survey Project on

---

[3] Alcopops have been defined by Babor et al. (2003) as a "relatively new form of alcoholic beverage characterised by carbonation, artificial colouring, sweetness, and sale by the 300ml bottle". The authors also point out that the marketing of alcopops has been criticised because of its potential attractiveness to children and young people. There is disagreement, however, regarding the role of alcopops in the drinking repertoires of teenagers, with some commentators claiming that the introduction of these beverages has contributed to an overall increase in alcohol consumption amongst the young (Roberts et al., 1999), and others questioning the legitimacy of this claim (Brain and Parker, 1997; Forsyth et al., 1997).

Alcohol and Other Drugs (ESPAD) studies (Hibell et al., 1997; 2000) confirm this shift towards a *style* of consumption characterised by heavy episodic drinking. Tables 6.1 and 6.2 illustrate the reported frequency of "being drunk in the last 30 days" and the reported frequency of "drinking five or more drinks in a row", based on the most recent ESPAD study of 16-year-old school-goers (Hibell et al., 2000).

Table 6.1: Frequency of Being Drunk in Last 30 days (number of occasions in the last 30 days)

	0	1–2	3–5	6–10	10–19	20–39	40+
Boys	51	22	15	15	7	1	1
Girls	50	28	14	6	2	1	0
All Pupils	50	25	15	6	2	1	0

Source: Hibell et al., 2000.

According to the data presented in Table 6.1, half of the study's 16-year-olds reported at least one occasion of drunkenness during the past 30 days; 25 per cent were drunk on 1-2 occasions, and 15 per cent on 3-5 occasions, during the past 30 days. These figures also indicate that girls were as likely as boys to report at least one episode of drunkenness in the past month. Looking then to the frequency of drinking five or more drinks in a row (Table 6.2) — a commonly used measure of binge drinking — 57 per cent of 16 year-old alcohol consumers reported this behaviour on at least one occasion during the past 30 days. Of these, 26 per cent did so on one to two occasions and 17 per cent on between three and five of their drinking episodes. Again, girls were as likely as boys to report drinking five or more drinks in a row.

Table 6.2: Frequency of Drinking Five or More Drinks in a Row
(number of occasions in the last 30 days)

	0	1–2	3–5	6–9	10+
Boys	43	26	17	10	5
Girls	44	25	18	9	5
All Pupils	43	26	17	9	50

Source: Hibell et al., 2000.

To summarise, available statistical data pertaining to alcohol consumption among school-going youth, spanning a 20-year-period, suggest that the main trends in drinking patterns are greater experimentation with alcohol and increases in "high-risk" drinking patterns such as binge drinking and drunkenness. The same can be said for the slightly older age group of 18-24-year-olds, who are more likely to engage in binge drinking (Ramstedt and Hope, 2004), but who drink less frequently than older age groups (Friel et al., 1999). This trend mirrors that in the UK, where large amounts of alcohol are consumed by the young weekly drinkers, who also drink more alcohol per session (Brain, 2002; Brain et al., 2000; Measham, 1996; Parker and Williams, 2003). Another significant trend in Ireland since the mid-1990s is the mixing of alcohol with other psychoactive substances including cannabis, ecstasy and cocaine (Mayock, 2000; 2001; 2002). Within a variety of social settings, "going out" increasingly holds the possibility of using illegal drugs. We know, for example, that drug consumption amongst Irish youth has risen steadily throughout the 1990s (Hibell et al., 1997; 2000), and that Ireland currently has one of the most drug experienced youth populations in the EU (EMCDDA, 2003). Recent claims regarding the pervasiveness of drug use amongst the young have emanated primarily from UK-based research, where researchers have described young people as "drug wise" (Parker et al., 1995) and "very drug experienced" (Measham et al., 2001). Two consecutive ESPAD studies (Hibell et al., 1997; 2000) have uncovered close similarities in drug use prevalence rates among 16-year-olds in Ireland and the UK. As noted by Parker (2001):

It is interesting that Ireland comes closer to the UK drugs profile than any other European country but there is no authoritative literature which attempts to explain this extraordinary status (p. 3).

Increasingly, it appears that alcohol — often described as the "favourite" drug of young people (Parker et al., 1998; Royal College of Psychiatrists, 1986) — is the mainstay of *broader psychoactive repertories*. Current drinking styles may, therefore, reflect a more general and widespread psychoactive culture amongst contemporary youth. This growing trend toward alcohol-based polydrug repertories has been noted across Europe (World Health Organisation, 2001; EMCDDA, 2003), where rates of drug use are much higher amongst the young and most prevalent among "the relatively affluent outgoing urban youth, with a key link between drugs and alcohol" (EMCDDA, 2002, p. 1).

It is important to point out that although there is widespread consensus amongst researchers about the potentially problematic nature of "binge drinking", and its distinctiveness from moderate drinking, there is no generally accepted definition of the term.[4] For example, Moore et al. (1994) defined an episode of binge drinking as the consumption of seven or more standard drinks for women and ten or more standard drinks for men. Nadeau et al. (1998) used eight standard drinks per day to define binge drinking, while Reilly et al. (1998) defined different levels of binge drinking in terms of risk. Low risk drinking was defined by Reilly et al. (1998) as 0-5 drinks for women and 0-6 drinks for men; hazardous drinking as 6-13 drinks for women and 7-14 drinks for men, while harmful use was 13 or more drinks for women and 15 or more drinks for men. A recent analysis of drinking culture and "binge" drinking in an Irish context estimated the frequency of drinking larger amounts of alcohol (i.e. binge drinking) by asking respondents to state how many times during the past 12 months they had consumed "at least one bottle of wine, 25 centilitres of spirits or four pints of beer, or more, during one drinking occasion" (Ramstedt and Hope, 2004). Irrespective of variations in definition, there

---

[4] It is also worth noting that different terminology has been used to describe this distinctive style of alcohol consumption. For example, Measham (1996) refers to "binge drinking" as *heavy sessional drinking*, while Murgraff et al. (1999) use the term *risky single-occasion drinking*.

is considerable agreement that binge drinking is a public health matter of considerable concern. The adverse effects of alcohol extend across many health domains; alcohol consumption not only impacts on physical and mental health but may also lead to an array of personal, social and financial difficulties. Alcohol-related mortality is high in Ireland, drink driving is a significant problem and alcohol contributes to a range of personal problems affecting relationships with family members, friends and work colleagues (Strategic Task-Force on Alcohol, 2002). Strong links have been found between alcohol and public order offences (National Crime Council, 2003), and the "risky" drinking habits of Irish drinkers are associated with many experiences of harmful drinking-related consequences, particularly among men (Ramstedt and Hope, 2003).

Contemporary Youth Lifestyles

Youth lifestyles have changed quite dramatically in the past 20 years. Changes in patterns of educational participation, delayed labour market transitions and an extension in the period of dependency have all had significant implications for the lifestyles young people adopt and for the ways in which they spend their free time (Furlong and Cartmel, 1997). In addition, the traditionally structuring features of lifelong occupations, class-based communities and patriarchal nuclear families are today weaker than at any time in the past. Many young people have better educational and career opportunities than their predecessors but these opportunities also bring higher levels of unpredictability and, with this, young people are charged with making a greater range of choices in may different aspects of life. As a consequence of these changes, young people, according to Furlong and Cartmel (1997), are charged with negotiating a set of risks largely unknown to their parents, irrespective of their social background or gender.

Contemporary societies are consumer societies (Featherstone, 1991) and, within emerging global economies, more and more emphasis falls on the consumption of goods as "culture".

Reviewing statistical data on the purchase of various consumable items, including alcohol, O'Connell (2001) has characterised recent changes in Irish society as indicative of rapid modernisation, with "rampant consumerism and individualism leading the charge". Today's teenagers grow up and live in a global economy, with the globalisation of media and markets increasingly shaping their perceptions, choices and behaviours. Young people are more likely than previously to be addressed as consumers and valued for their roles as customers, patrons and clients (Palladion, 1996). Indeed, contemporary youth appear to have particularly well-developed needs for aesthetic consumption and are able, at least superficially, to construct themselves as consumer citizens, through distinctive purchasing styles and patterns of consumption. Wyn and White (1997, pp. 86-87) go as far as to suggest that, "youth itself is a consumable item"; it can be purchased on every high street in the form of clothing, footwear, music, leisure activities, mobile phones, alcohol and other psychoactive substances. One could argue that *consuming pleasure* has become central to youth cultural forms at the turn of the century. According to Brain (2002):

> [Consumer societies] are societies whose justification rests on the individual right to consume and the promotion of the notion that the good life is to be gained through these goods and services we consume. They encourage societies of instant gratification in which the pleasures of consumption are both material and symbolic (p. 5).

How and what we consume, as Tovey and Share (2000) note, makes up much of what we conceptualise as culture; in consuming goods, "we consume culture and we also create and re-create it" (p. 428). The claim that the contemporary social world we inhabit is centrally a world of consumption (Featherstone, 1991) underlies many recent analyses of the contemporary world of youthful drug use (Collison, 1996; Measham et al., 2001; Parker et al., 1998; Taylor, 2000; van Ree, 2002). Within this emergent literature, illicit drug use has come to be associated with youth consumer lifestyles (EMCDDA, 2002). This conceptualisation can be applied equally to alcohol, which is clearly a versatile and *legal* commodity subject to a continually evolving and dynamic relationship between supply and demand (Stockwell and Crosbie, 2001).

Consuming Youth and the Alcohol Market

While many young people today have greater opportunities and more disposable income, they are simultaneously more vulnerable to selling and marketing techniques that have become more aggressive for consumer products (WHO, 2001). Children and young people are increasingly becoming target groups for aggressive marketing practices with a view to stimulating and increasing the consumption of a wide range of leisure/pleasure products. The alcohol industry, like any other commercial enterprise, is not naïve to the economics of pleasure. It is, in fact, claimed that as early as the 1980s, the drinks industry began to target a new generation of young drinkers, both male and female, who demanded a greater range of alcohol products and different kinds of drinking venue from the traditional pub (Coffield and Gofton, 1994).[5] Among other strategies, this entailed efforts on the part of the industry to establish a stronger presence in the everyday lives and minds of potential customers. During the past decade, the drinks industry in Ireland has, for example, increased its visibility through the sponsorship of many sporting and cultural activities (Strategic Task-Force on Alcohol, 2002). Mass media is, of course, one of the most ubiquitous sources of normative support for drinking (Grube and Morgan, 1990).

The findings of a recently published study of the effects of alcohol advertising on Irish teenagers demonstrate that alcohol advertising has a strong attraction for young people, which they perceive as upholding a lifestyle and image to which they aspire (Dring and Hope, 2001). Efforts such as these on the part of the alcohol industry to respond to changing youth lifestyles are unsurprising from a marketing perspective, since the

---

[5] Collin (1997) argues that the extent of the transformation of youthful leisure and pleasure landscapes brought about by the rise to prominence of rave culture coincided with falling alcohol sales and diminishing attendance in pubs during the early 1990s. This did not go unnoticed by the brewing industry which, he asserts, "began to worry that the shift may be irrevocable, a nascent nation of teetotallers fuelled by pills, powders and puff, drinking only Lucozade and Evian water" (p. 273). According to Brain (2000), the drinks industry has been "spectacularly successful in recapturing the 'rave' market" (p. 3). From this perspective, the expansion in recreational drug use has been critical to redefining how the alcohol industry relates to the youth market, providing customised need satisfaction through a choice of "designer" drinks in an attempt to keep pace with the recreational drug scene.

profitability of the alcohol industry logically requires the continual recruitment of new generations of young drinkers. Alcohol is now a highly diversified product with a spectrum of prices and a broader range of products than in the past (Ponicki et al., 1995). Internationally, the past decade in particular has seen the production and distribution of alcoholic beverages become concentrated in fewer and bigger enterprises where the assortment of beverage types and brands has been expanded alongside vigorous efforts to market them (Jackson et al., 2000; Partanen and Simpuura, 2001). A number of key transformations within the alcohol market, including the drinking environments that support it, can be summarised as follows:

- The alcohol market has *diversified*. In doing so, it has sought out new ways of capturing the interest and imagination of young drinkers who, they hope, will remain loyal to their products. A wide range of new alcohol beverages (ice lagers, spirit mixers, ciders and alcopops) has been released and many existing products have been "re-commodified". Collectively known as "designer drinks" (Brain and Parker, 1998), many of these beverages are marketed in large part for their "buzz" or "hit" value.

- Alcohol products are increasingly advertised as *lifestyle markers* (Brain, 2000) in which branding and product image plays a central role. Sophisticated advertising campaigns have been developed in a drive to create market niches for a wide range of "branded" products, in the form of pre-mixed cocktails and other "designer" drinks. Dring and Hope's (2001) recent research on the effects of alcohol advertising on young people illustrates this point very well; the study's teenagers associated many alcoholic products with pleasure, fun, and with cool and sophisticated places and people. There was also evidence to suggest that young people believed particular beverages and brands to have sexual currency.

- Ireland has a well-established pub culture. It currently has the largest population of "out of home" drinkers throughout Europe (Babor et al., 2003), generating a range of potential demands to which the alcohol industry has responded efficiently. A whole new range of bars, theme pubs and club bars have been opened in an attempt to create settings that are attractive to a large and diverse population of youth consumers. The rise to prominence of the "super pub" in Ireland is one of the most notable developments within drinking settings over the past ten years. In many densely populated urban areas, the traditional pub has been replaced by pseudo-club settings that facilitate larger numbers of people; these drinking settings might be justifiably described as frenetic social environments that encourage excess rather than moderation.[6]

The drinks industry has clearly come to see contemporary young drinkers as a *diverse group*, many of them with repertoires of alcohol- (and drug-) related experiences, as well as diverse tastes in terms of what they consume, where, and why. Ireland's large youth population has provided a natural-born growth sector for the alcohol industry.[7] The availability and popularity of non-alcoholic mixer beverages — containing legal stimulants such as caffeine — is a particularly significant development. In pubs and clubs these drinks are combined with alcohol, providing, as will be demonstrated in the presentation of empirical data, cocktails that are valued primarily for their "buzz" value.[8] Other so-called "brand-in-hand" products offer the benefits of strength, flavour and portability (MacKintosh et al., 1997). The branding of a range of new "designer drinks" since the early 1990s — including "Bacardi Breezer", "WKD" and "FCUK" to name but a few — exemplifies the industry's efforts to target and seduce the youth population with appealing "young" drinks with a "buzz" value. These strategies are endemic to consumer capitalism which, it is claimed, plays a central role in the marketing of drug referenced products to young people as part of their leisure and lifestyle (Blackman, 1996).

---

[6] The rise to prominence of the "superpub" can be partly explained by the licensing legislation in Ireland. Because no new pub licences have been issued, existing pub owners have extended their premises (in some cases, creating 3-4 floors of drinking space) to cater for a growing population of young drinkers.

[7] Although the 2002 Population Census indicated a slight decline in the youth population, the population of 15-19, 20-24 and 25-29-year-olds rose steadily between 1971 and 1996 (Central Statistics Office, 2002).

[8] At the time of writing, the Department of Health and Children was reviewing its policy on stimulant drinks in the wake of a European Court of Justice decision to uphold the French Government's ban on Red Bull, one of the most popular caffeine-based stimulant drinks on the market (Healy, 2004).

Today's Young Drinkers

The remainder of this chapter draws on empirical data collected during a longitudinal ethnographic study of drug use among young people in an inner-city Dublin community. The study site was selected on the basis of having a strong drugs culture and a history of concentrated drug problems. The methodology has been described in detail elsewhere (Mayock, 2003) and may be reviewed there; the following is a brief overview of some of the most salient methodological features of the study. Individual in-depth interviews and focus group discussions, coupled with prolonged participation with the study site, were the primary methods of data collection. The study was longitudinal and conducted in two phases; the first in 1998 and a follow-up phase in 2001. Fifty-seven young people aged between 15 and 19 years were recruited into the study in 1998. Study participants were categorised as "abstainers", "drugtakers" and "problem drugtakers", respectively, in accordance with their own perception of their drug use status at the time of conducting Phase I interviews.[9] Contact was re-established with 42 of the study's participants in 2001, at which stage they ranged in age from 18 to 23 years. During Phase II interviews, young people were again questioned about their drug use status, with the majority reporting modifications to their drug use practices since the initial interview. For example, one-third of the study's Phase II "abstainers" reported the transition to illicit drug consumption at the time of their follow-up interview in 2001. Although illicit drug use was a major focus of the investigation, research participants were asked detailed questions about their alcohol consumption during both phases of the study. All were questioned about their early drinking experiences, the settings where they consumed alcohol (both as teenagers and young adults), the regularity of their drinking, the types of beverages they consumed and their preferred drinks and drinking settings. The study's

---

[9] "Abstainers" are non-users of illicit drugs; they abstain from illegal drugs but *not* from alcohol; "drugtakers" are young people who use drugs recreationally but do not consider their drug use to be problematic; finally, "problem drugtakers" are young people who use "hard" drugs (i.e., heroin and/or cocaine) and they consider their drug consumption to be problematic. All of the participating young people self-nominated as "abstainers", "drugtakers" or "problem drugtakers", in accordance with how *they* perceived the nature of their drug consumption.

longitudinal focus permitted changes in respondents' patterns of drinking to be traced through their teenage years into young adulthood.

The study yielded a wealth of data on young people's lifestyles, social activities, peer and romantic relationships, their drug- and other risk-taking behaviours, as well as a diverse range of views and perspectives on both legal and illegal psychoactive substance use. However, it is data pertaining to alcohol consumption and related lifestyle characteristics that are the primary focus of this analysis. Selected data are drawn from the accounts of the study's abstainers (from drugs) and drugtakers only.[10] The vast majority of these young people sampled their first alcoholic drink before the age of 13 years. From this, they progressed to more regular drinking patterns and, by the mid-teenage years, the majority were weekly drinkers. It should be stressed from the outset that, for a large number, alcohol consumption was connected in important ways to illicit drug use. The psychoactive repertories of the study's drug users (including "abstainers" who made the transition to drug use by the time of conducting Phase II interviews) were dominated by alcohol and cannabis. Stimulant drugs, including ecstasy, amphetamine and cocaine, were extensively used but not with the degree of regularity and consistency reported in the case of alcohol and cannabis. Importantly, these young people did not consider their alcohol or drug consumption to be unusual or problematic, and they consistently described their drug-related activities as "social" or "recreational". Finally, practically all were generally conformist in their lifestyle choices. Although a significant proportion left school before completing their formal education, the vast majority were either employed in a full- or part-time capacity or in the process of completing a training programme or apprenticeship by the time of their Phase II interview. Practically all lived at home with their parent(s), making a financial contribution to the household on a weekly basis.

---

[10] The study's problem drugtakers struggled with a range of problems and issues related to the problematic nature of their heroin consumption and, at the stage of conducting Phase II interviews, only one described herself as "drug free". For the majority, alcohol was not a strong feature of their psychoactive repertories, particularly during more chaotic periods of heavy drug consumption. Problem drugtakers were highly marginalised: they did not socialise with "recreational" drug users, they remained tightly bound to their home neighbourhood and their social networks comprised, for the most part, of other "heavy end" drug users who were deeply enmeshed in local heroin scenes.

There is no claim that these data are representative of the views and experiences of the entire youth population. Rather, the intention is to establish an empirically based flavour of what it *means* to consume alcohol within contemporary youth drinking scenes. The overall aim is to construct a qualitative picture of the role which alcohol consumption plays in young people's "going out" rituals and routines. The primary focus, therefore, is on the *way* young drinkers articulate the benefits of alcohol consumption, rather than on quantifying the amounts they consume weekly or on any one drinking occasion.

Drinking Settings/Drinking Styles

Over the course of the study, young people described a range of drinking settings. For example, younger teenagers who could not gain admittance to licensed premises usually drank at outdoor locations. Known colloquially as "knacker" drinking, outdoor alcohol consumption provided a unique set of rewards. As adult-free social spaces, these settings permitted young people to create their own leisure arenas using minimal material resources. The only requirement was the presence of friends, and enough money to buy "a few cans"; a portable sound system, if available, was a bonus. Considerations of cost, availability and maximum effect, rather than preferences for specific drinks, determined young people's early choices of alcoholic beverages:

> I would have tried anything that was cheap, you know, 'cause like a bottle of cider was like £2.50 or something, you know what I mean. And when you drink that you would be locked like. So any cheap drink like that you could afford is what you would get. At that stage we would all probably be drunk on a few cans (Female, 18 years).

Heavy sessional outdoor drinking emerged as a significant social activity for a large number during their early to mid-teens. Elements of "unbounded lifestyles" (Brain et al., 2000), where excessive consumption and offending behaviour merged, resonated from a minority of the study's early drinkers. One young woman explained that this teenage "mad game", involving street-based alcohol and drug use, incorporated "delinquent" activity in the form of vandalism and petty crime.

At the time when we were out drinking an' all that I used to see it as big, like, years ago. All me friends and the fellas. We used to smash cars and rob radios to get our money an' all. It's a mad game (Female, 19.9 years).

By the age of 17 or 18, pubs and clubs were the desired settings in which to spend weekend nights out. The majority had outgrown street drinking and several regarded the activity as a mark of immaturity:

I wouldn't drink a can out on the street now. I'd be ashamed of my life. I am not into it anymore. It's stupid. You are just making a show of yourself. I just copped on. I wouldn't drink out now, none of us would drink out anymore.

The move into pub and club settings generally signalled the end of street drinking and this transition also marked a changed role for alcohol. The vast majority of the study's abstainers and drugtakers had established regular drinking patterns by the age of 18 and practically all reported a dramatic increase in the frequency and intensity of their alcohol consumption as they neared their late teenage years. These developments were closely related to young people's transition from school (or training) to the workforce and their more regular attendance at city-centre pubs and clubs. A large number socialised outside of their home neighbourhoods and travelled to the city-centre, particularly on weekends. The "super pubs" and clubs that they frequented were demanding environments in their own right and, consequently, their nights out required a degree of advance planning. The following account was told by a regular patron of city-centre pubs and clubs. As a drinker who perceived himself to have "a high tolerance for alcohol", he partly attributed his regular "binge" drinking to the practicalities of navigating crowded city-centre social setting:

Well, the one thing I will say is that whenever (pause) . . . if we do go out in a big gang, the way I think Dublin is now at the minute, or the clubs in Dublin are with the crowds that go to them; if you don't go to a club early you're not going to get in and you are going to struggle. And people don't want to stand in a queue for an hour, or I certainly don't. So the way I look at it is that I think I have to go into town at 8.30 to get into a club. And you obviously drink a lot more if you go into town at 8.30 than you would

> if you go in at 10.30 or 11.00. And there has been nights when you would drink inhuman amounts . . . (Male, age 22).

Young people — women and men alike — enjoyed socialising in crowded bars and clubs. Being part of the city's vibrant social scene was important to the majority, even if many could not afford to socialise in the city-centre every weekend. Young people almost always described their nights out in positive terms. However, reports of unexpected negative events did emerge, particularly from regular patrons of late night bars and clubs. Many, for example, had observed fights both inside and outside clubs on their nights out and a smaller number — primarily young men — were themselves victims of assault in these settings.

> At the time, now, it didn't seem like much. I remember standin' on the street and then I was away from me mates and the next thing I get this punch in the face . . . I don't remember gettin' home but the next day I had a black eye. And I was like, fuck, what am I goin' to tell me ma? (Male, 20 years).

When questioned about the number of alcoholic beverages typically consumed, the "losing count" factor featured strongly in young people's accounts. However, several openly admitted to having consumed volumes of alcohol far exceeding their tolerance level. Many were unable to estimate the number of alcoholic beverages they drank on a night out and stated openly that they simply lost count as the night progressed. This is interesting, since practically all who used illicit drugs knew precisely how much they were likely to consume over the course of a typical night. For the majority of young people, consuming alcohol was central to having a good time — most commonly expressed as "having the craic" — in a variety of social settings. Alcohol consumption was integral to going out and its legitimacy and acceptability was at no stage questioned; on the contrary, it was described as "normal", "sociable" or an "everyday thing".

Drinking for a "Buzz"

A principal reason for drinking was to get drunk, or, in the language of young people themselves, to get a "buzz". Phrases like "drinking gives me a high" and "you get out of it on drink" were commonly deployed to convey the benefits of alcohol consumption. In this style of drinking, the utility of alcohol is increasingly centred on its hit value. It was clear that for a large number — probably the majority — drinking was valued not simply as a social facilitator but because of its psychoactive properties:

> Yeah, I do love goin' out drinking and I love gettin' locked. I don't do it during the week but at the weekend, yeah, love to go out with me friends, go dancin' an' all that. We all meet up on a Saturday night fairly early, head into town.
>
> [Do you go to pubs?]
>
> Yeah, go to a pub first and then head to a club. It does be all hours when we get home. In bits the next day after the drink but it's worth it (Male, 22 years).

There was little difference between the study's young women and men in terms of their general orientation towards alcohol; alcohol consumption played a central role in their social lives and both stressed the importance of their Friday and Saturday nights out. However, young men were more likely to describe their drinking as "heavy" or excessive. Some gender differences also emerged in the types of alcohol beverages consumed. A large number of young men drank lager, although a number frequently switched to spirits or alcopops as the night progressed, particularly if their drinking was club-based. Young women, on the other hand, were more likely to drink spirits or alcoholic fruit drinks and/or to use high-energy beverages as mixers. Vodka and Red Bull was an extremely popular cocktail, consumed by some as a preferred drink and by others as an "upper" as the night went on. This young woman, like many others, praised Red Bull for the extra "buzz" or "high", in a manner similar to the study's stimulant drug users.

> I'd drink about four bottles of Smirnoff Ice and then I'd start going on to the vodka and Red Bull. That makes me hyper, the Red Bull. I just am as high as a kite. I don't be locked, falling around. I'd be just real giddy, real hyper, real energy, loads of energy because I do be wrecked after work because every first week of the month I work from half eight until seven o'clock, Monday to Friday. And I do be wrecked and I just need something to give me energy at the end of the week. So I just drink that (Female, 19.9 years).

For many young drinkers, the benefits of drinking "for a buzz" converged around "time out", winding down after the week's work and having a good time, as illustrated in the following account.

> I go out as much as I can. I love being out, you know that kind of way. I love staying in as well, love my nights in. But you work so hard during the week, you know what I mean? . . . I like to just start off with a couple of bottles of Miller and then I would probably have a few vodkas and that then. I would be twisted then. I love getting' twisted. I probably drink a lot when I'm out. I just go out and have a laugh on the weekends, ya know (Female, 21 years).

The combination of working long hours and the desire to maintain a hectic social life appeared to strongly influence the use of high-strength "brand in hand" designer drinks. For a large number of young people in full-time employment, the working week was followed by a weekend of socialising on alcohol, a style of alcohol consumption similar to that described by Measham (1996) as a "big bang" approach for maximum impact. Different drinks were associated with different types of rewards, and the manner in which they combined lager, spirits, mixers and "brand in hand" products is highly suggestive of a conscious and deliberate attempt to gain the maximum benefit from an evening out. In the following account, perceived benefit is closely equated with a desired level of intoxication.

> I drink more than I used to. I suppose it's to relax, take it easy, have a bit of craic after the week at work. If I went out and started drinking Smirnoff Ice all night that wouldn't get me drunk, wouldn't do anything for me. Whereas if you go out and have say a couple of pints of Budweiser and then go on to vodka and Red Bull, you're going to be drunk (Male, 22.5 years).

This search for pleasurable "time out" was a distinctive feature of the young people's narratives. During the week, they led a fairly conventional life — they worked hard to earn money to maintain themselves and finance everyday needs; at the weekend, the pursuit of pleasure and instant gratification took hold for large numbers. For the most part, young people depicted their nights out as fulfilling, positive and worthwhile. Alcohol consumption was costly from a financial point of view and, at times, the repercussions were difficult because of severe hangovers. However, these factors were easily dismissed as the following weekend approached.

Alcohol-based Polydrug Repertories

As stated earlier, the practice of combining alcohol with illegal drugs was widespread. Illicit drugs were combined with alcohol by a large numbers of the study's young people for the attainment of maximum fulfilment in the form of a "buzz" or "high". Stimulant drug users usually started off the night with alcohol and later added a preferred substance (ecstasy, amphetamine or cocaine) for the achievement of a desired effect. For many, these combinations simply made the night last longer.

> Goin' out drinking, well, I usually take something else as well. Especially at weekends. If ya take E or speed, ya get a great buzz and ya can keep goin' all night. Ya won't get as tired as with drink on its own. So I usually take something with drink when I go clubbing (Female, 20.5 years).

Purposive "mixing" was widespread and, in general, young people's drug and alcohol combinations were carefully chosen. Among those who snorted cocaine powder, for example, on some (although rarely all) of their nights out, alcohol was a critical cocktail ingredient.

> I did coke for the first time when I was 19. It's a completely different buzz. You feel good for 15 minutes and then its gone and you're like, 'Give me more', or whatever. But it's totally different . . . I thought it was great. You think you're a king walking around clubs. Drink like a fish. Coke is very good with drink (Male, 21.5 years).

The interrelationship between alcohol and illicit drugs is clearly important for understanding the going-out sector's nights out. Alcohol emerged as an essential "mixer" for recreational drug users, irrespective of what they nominated as their drug of choice. Moreover, as many "grew out" of heavier periods of drug consumption, they increasingly nominated alcohol as their "favourite" drug.

> I used ta be more into the E and speed, especially E. It was a great buzz but then I got a bit sick of it. I couldn't be bothered as much now. I usually stick to the drink. It's better anyway (Female, 19.5 years).

It is important to state that among those interviewed there were more moderate drinkers who were far more cautious in their approach to alcohol. Furthermore, not all of the study's young drinkers consumed alcohol purely for its "hit" value. While the majority emphasised the sociability and, indeed, the normality of drinking for fun and pleasure, several described a far more cautious approach to alcohol:

> I never go over three drinks 'cos I see these others and I'd never like to be in the state they're in. I don't know me limits and I wouldn't like to find out. I'm happy with my three. In fact, I'm happy with two (Female, 17 years).

These young people were less likely to be illicit drug users and/or to socialise regularly in city-centre pubs and clubs. They typically earned less and their social life was more likely to involve drinking locally with friends and family members.

Conclusion

A central premise of this chapter is that it is neither reasonable nor meaningful to talk about "binge" drinking or, for that matter, other styles of alcohol consumption, without reference to the social and economic environments that support them. As these environments change, so too do the behaviours within them. The *Interim Report* of the Strategic Task Force on Alcohol (2002) identified increased affluence, the relative decline in alcohol taxes, and increased availability as factors that have influenced the sharp growth in alcohol consumption levels in Ireland. This analysis has attempted to speak to the phenomenon of binge drinking amongst the young with reference to wider social, economic and cultural changes that inevitably impact on aspects of young people's lives, including the lifestyles and leisure/pleasure arenas available to them.

The life experiences of contemporary youth have changed dramatically and recent years have seen a growth in the value youth culture attaches to consumer goods. Brand labels — whether those placed on clothing, footwear, T-shirts, badges, music or posters — have strong material and symbolic significance. The alcohol industry has responded to the diverse leisure demands of contemporary youth by designing an expansive range of products that cater for variable tastes, lifestyles and changed orientations to "going out". In so doing, it has provided young drinkers with an expansive cocktail cabinet of alcoholic products. The empirical data presented in this chapter suggest that young people have embraced lifestyles that prioritise the pursuit of consumable pleasure. We have seen, for example, how they purchase branded products for precisely the reasons emphasised in the industry's promotional campaigns. Another striking feature of their narratives is their "pick and mix" approach (Measham et al., 1994) to psychoactive substance use. Much of the "talk" centred on the "hit" value of certain alcoholic drinks, with so-called "designer drinks" and "ready to drink" branded products featuring strongly in young people's combination-approach to single episodes of heavy consumption. In this style of consumption, drinking to intoxication is of crucial significance. Their drinking occasions may well result in difficult hangovers and, in fewer instances, intoxication fuels verbal and/or physical altercations on the street. However, the majority of young people whose drinking and drug use "stories" are told in this chapter display a generally conformist approach to life and living and are, in fact, ensconced in lives that otherwise anchor them to the social order. Put differently, they embrace a work hard/play hard ideology (Parker and Williams, 2003) that permits them to "let loose" at the weekends. This mix of hedonism and conservatism may appear contradictory. However, in a world where consumption is omnipresent, young people are essentially conservative in their approach to life (Miles, 2000). Alcohol (and drug) consumption offer ways of temporarily escaping or defying the tedium of the ordinary; using this lens, the emphasis moves to hyperreality and consumption becomes a dominant form of social expression (Featherstone, 1987).

Alcohol, to borrow the expression of Babor et al. (2003), is clearly *no ordinary commodity*.

The societal consequences of "binge" or "high-risk" drinking will only be fully realised in the future. Nonetheless, we already know that the adverse effects of alcohol extend beyond physical health issues to mental, social and financial problems (Strategic Task Force on Alcohol, 2002). The binge drinking phenomenon is highly unlikely to disappear given the size and "outgoing" orientation of our youth population. Moreover, the drink industry's sustained efforts to promote and expand its range of products continues to fuel an already well-established drinking culture that prizes excess over moderation, certainly amongst the young.

All of this raises challenging questions about what Brain (2002) refers to as "sustainable consumption", that is, forms of consumption that do not undermine the ability of individuals or groups to sustain the roles and functions that living in contemporary society demands. The alcohol industry continues to extol the merits of *education* which, it claims, will promote a better understanding among young people of the dangers of drinking to excess, thereby reducing harm among risk groups. This is despite consistent evidence that education programmes do not impact significantly — if at all — on the alcohol-related behaviour of youth or, indeed, of other sectors of the population (Strategic Task Force on Alcohol, 2002). Meanwhile, we have a National Alcohol Policy since 1996 offering a clear set of public health measures aimed at curbing alcohol consumption rates. This remains unimplemented. As Butler (2003) points out, the establishment of the Strategic Task Force on Alcohol in 2002 means that we now effectively have two parallel alcohol policy processes, one based in the Department of Justice, Equality and Law Reform and, the second based at the Department of Health and Children. The former is dominated by the interest groups (including the drinks industry), which are committed primarily to consumerism and have only a minority public health voice, whereas the latter *is* the voice of the public health perspective on alcohol. This situation is wholly undesirable, not least because of their contrasting approaches to the alcohol use phenomenon. We have, in effect, no integrated or "joined-up" approach to alcohol and no single Government department with overall responsibility for the implementation of a national alcohol policy (Butler, 2002). Meanwhile, what is clear is that the issues and problems arising from alcohol consumption, both in general and youth populations, are not about to fade. While one may optimistically speculate that it is a minority of individuals who are binge drinkers and risk-takers, it is overall alcohol consumption rates that drive up the cost of excess to the public purse (Strategic Task Force on Alcohol, 2002). Two challenging questions immediately arise out of the current acrimonious debate on alcohol policy: Will the Government challenge the vested interests of a powerful and well-resourced alcohol industry? And, in the event of such a radical move, will the public and young drinkers, in particular, favour a seemingly more punitive approach to their lifestyle choices?

References

Babor, T.F., Caetano, R., Casswell, S., Edwards, G., Giesbrecht, N., Graham, K., Grube, J., Gruenedwald, P., Hill, L., Holder, H., Homel, R., Österberg, E., Rehm, J., Room R. and Rossow, I. (2003) *Alcohol: No Ordinary Commodity — Research and Public Policy*. Oxford and London: Oxford University Press.

Blackman, S. (1996) "Has drug culture become an inevitable part of youth culture? A critical assessment of drug education". *Educational Review*, 48, 2, 131-142.

Brain, K.J. (2002) *Youth, Alcohol, and the Emergence of the Post-modern Alcohol Order*. Occasional Paper No.1. London: Institute of Alcohol Studies.

Brain, K. and Parker, H. (1997) *Drinking With Design: Alcopops, Designer Drinks and Youth Culture*. London: Portman Publications.

Brain, K., Parker, H. and Carnwath, T. (2000) "Drinking with design: young drinkers as psychoactive consumers". *Drugs: education, prevention and policy*, 7, 1, 5-20.

Brown, V. (2003) "The demon drink is a killer virus". *Irish Times*, 30 April.

Butler, S. (2002) *How Local is Local? A Reflection on Recent Irish Attempts to Create Alcohol Policy*. Paper presented at the 2rd Annual Conference of the Addiction Research Centre: "Debating Public Policies on Drugs and Alcohol". 26 September 2002, Trinity College, Dublin.

Butler, S. (2003) "Paying the price for extended opening hours: a comment from Ireland". *Drugs: education, prevention and policy*, 10, 4, 293-296.

Cassidy, E. (2003) "Young Irish biggest binge drinkers". *Irish Examiner*, 9 October 2003.

Cassidy, T. (1997) "Alcoholism in Ireland". In A. Cleary and M.P. Treacy (eds.) *The Sociology of Health and Illness in Ireland*. Dublin: University of Dublin Press. pp. 175-192.

Central Statistics Office (2002) *Census 2002: Principal Demographic Results*. Dublin: Central Statistics Office.

Coffield, F. and Gofton, L. (1994) *Drugs and Young People*. London: Institute for Public Policy Research.

Collin, M. (1997) *Altered State: The Story of Ecstasy Culture and Acid House*. London: Serpent's Tail.

Collison, M. (1996) "In search of the high life: drugs, crime, masculinities and consumption". *British Journal of Criminology*, 36, 3, 428-444.

Dean, A. (1990) "Culture and community: drink and soft drugs in Hebridean youth culture". *Sociological Review*, 517-563.

Donnellan, E. (2003a) "Survey shows increasing binge drinking". *Irish Times*, 16 April 2003.

Donnellan, E. (2003b) "High alcohol levels in women in assault unit". *Irish Times*, 17 May 2003.

Dring, C. and Hope, A. (2001) *The Impact of Alcohol Advertising on Teenagers in Ireland*. Dublin: Department of Health and Children.

EMCDDA (2002) *Recreational Drug Use — a Key EU Challenge*. Drugs in Focus, Briefings 6. Lisbon: European Monitoring Centre for Drugs and Drug Addiction.

EMCDDA (2003) *Annual Report on the State of the Drugs Problem in the European Union and Norway*. Lisbon: European Monitoring Centre for Drugs and Drug Addiction.

Featherstone, M. (1987) "Lifestyle and consumer culture". *Theory, Culture and Society*, 4, 55-70.

Featherstone, M. (1991) *Consumer Culture and Postmodernism*. London: Sage Publications.

Forsyth, A.J.M., Barnard, M. and McKeganey, N.P. (1997) "Alcopop supernove: are alcoholic lemonades responsible for under-age drunkenness?" *International Journal of Health Education*, 35, 53-58.

Friel, S., Nic Gabhainn, S. and Kelleher, C. (1999) *The National Health and Lifestyle Surveys. Dublin and Galway*: Health Promotion Unit, Department of Health and Children, Dublin and Centre for Health Promotion Studies, NUI, Galway.

Furlong, A. and Cartmel, F. (1997) *Young People and Social Change: Individualization and Risk in Late Modernity*. Buckingham: Open University Press.

Grube, J. and Morgan, M. (1986) *Smoking, Drinking and Other Drug Use Among Dublin Post-Primary Pupils*. Dublin: The Economic and Social Research Institute. General Research Series, Paper 132.

Grube, J. and Morgan, M. (1990) *The Development and Maintenance of Smoking, Drinking and Other Drug Use Among Dublin Post-primary Pupils*. Dublin: The Economic and Social Research Institute. General Research Series, Paper 148.

Healy, A. (2004) "Red Bull ban in France for 10 years". *Irish Times*, 17 February 2004.

Hibell, B., Andersson, B. Ahlstrom, S., Balakireva, O., Bjarnasson, T., Kokkevi, A. and Morgan, M. (2000) *The 1999 ESPAD Report: Alcohol and Other Drug Use Among Students in 30 European Countries*. Stockholm: Council of Europe, Pompidou Group.

Hibell, B., Andersson, B., Bjarnason, T., Kokkevie, A., Morgan, M. and Narusk, A. (1997) *The 1995 ESPAD Report: Alcohol and Other Drug Use among Students in 26 European Countries*. Stockholm: Council of Europe, Pompidou Group.

Holmquist, K. (2003) "Drowning in drink". *Irish Times*, 1 April 2003.

Jackson, M.C., Hastings, G., Wheeler, C., Eadie, D. and Mackintosh, A.M. (2000) "Marketing alcohol to young people: implications for industry regulation and research policy". *Addiction*, 95 (Supplement 4), S597-S608.

Kelleher, C., NicGabhainn, S., Friel, S., Corrigan, H., Nolan, G., Sixsmith, J., Walsh, O. and Cooke, M. (2003) *The National Health and Lifestyle Surveys*. Health Promotion Unit, Department of Health and Children, Dublin and Centre for Health Promotion Studies, NUI, Galway.

MacKintosh, A.M., Hastings, G.B., Hughes, K., Wheeler, C., Watson, J. and Inglis, J. (1997) "Adolescent drinking – the role of designer drinks". *Health Education*, 6, 213-224.

Mayock, P. (2000) *Choosers or Losers? Influences on Young People's Choices about Drugs in Inner-city Dublin*. Dublin: The Children's Research Centre, Trinity College Dublin.

Mayock, P. (2001) "Cocaine use in Ireland: an exploratory study". In R. Moran, L. Dillon, M. O' Brien, P. Mayock, E. Farrell, with B. Pike *A Collection of Papers on Drug Issues in Ireland*. Dublin: Health Research Board. pp. 80-152.

Mayock, P. (2002) "Drug pathways, transitions and decisions: the experiences of young people in an inner-city Dublin community". *Contemporary Drug Problems*, 29, 1, 117-156.

Mayock, P. (2003) *Young People, Drugs and Risk: An Ethnography of Drug Use in a Dublin Inner-City Community.* Unpublished PhD Thesis, Social Studies Department, Trinity College, Dublin.

Measham, F. (1996) "The 'big bang' approach to sessional drinking: changing patterns of alcohol consumption amongst young people in North West England". *Addiction Research*, 4, 3, 283-299.

Measham, F., Aldridge, J. and Parker, H. (2001) *Dancing on Drugs: Risk, Health and Hedonism in the British Club Scene.* London: Free Association Books.

Miles, S. (2000) *Youth Lifestyles in a Changing World.* Buckingham: Open University Press.

Moore, L., Smith, C. and Catford, J. (1994) "Binge drinking: prevalence, patterns and policy". *Health Education Research*, 9, 4, 497-505.

Morgan, M. (2003) *Trends in Alcohol and Drug Use Amongst the Young.* Paper presented at the 3rd Annual Conference of the Addiction Research Centre: "The Substance of Youth: Alcohol and Drug Use among Young People". 4 September 2003, Trinity College, Dublin.

Morgan, M. and Grube, J. (1994) *Drinking among Dublin Post-primary School Pupils.* Dublin ESRI Genera Publications.

Morgan, M. and Grube, J.W. (1997) "Correlates of change in adolescent alcohol consumption in Ireland: implications for understanding influences and enhancing interventions". *Substance Use and Misuse*, 32, 5, 609-619.

Murgraff, B., Parrott, A., and Bennett, P. (1999) "Risky single-occasion drinking amongst young people – definition, correlates, policy and intervention: a broad overview of research findings". *Alcohol and Alcoholism*, 34, 1, 3-14.

National Alcohol Policy, Ireland (1996) Dublin: Stationery Office.

National Crime Council (2003) *Public Order Offences in Ireland.* Dublin: Stationery Office.

Nadeau, L., Guyon, L. and Bourgault, C. (1998) "Heavy drinkers in the general population: comparison of two measures". *Addiction Research*, 6, 2, 165-188.

O'Brien, C. (2003) "Young binge drinkers show signs of sclerosis". *Irish Examiner*, 21 March 2003.

O'Connell, M. (2001) *Changed Utterly: Ireland and the New Irish Psyche.* Dublin: The Liffey Press.

O'Connor, J. (1978) *The Young Drinkers: A Cross-National Study of Social and Cultural Influences*. London: Tavistock Publications.

O'Riordan, S. (2002)" Drunken binges 'fuel violence on streets'". *Irish Examiner*, 5 March 2002.

Palladion, G. (1996) *Teenagers: An American History*. New York: Basic Books.

Parker, H. (2001) "Unbelievable? The UK's drug present". In H. Parker, J. Aldridge and R. Egginton (eds.) *UK Drugs Unlimited: New Research and Policy Lessons on Illicit Drug Use*. New York: Palgrave. pp. 1-13.

Parker, H., Aldridge, J. and Measham, F. (1998) *Illegal Leisure: The Normalization of Adolescent Recreational Drug Use*. London: Routledge.

Parker, H., Measham, F. and Aldridge, J. (1995) *Drug Futures: Changing Patterns of Drug Use Amongst English Youth*. ISDD Research Monograph Seven. London: Institute for the Study of Drug Dependence.

Parker, H. and Williams, L. (2003) "Intoxicated weekends: young adults' work hard-play hard lifestyles, public health and public disorder". *Drug: education, prevention and policy*, 10, 4, 345-367.

Partanen, J. and Simpuura, J.P. (2001) "International trends in alcohol production and consumption". In N. Heather, T.J. Peters and T. Stockwell (eds.) *International Handbook of Alcohol Dependence and Problems*. Chichester, England: John Wiley and Sons Ltd. pp. 379-394.

Ponicki, W., Holder, H., Gruenewald, P. and Romelsjo, A. (1995) "Altering alcohol price by ethanol content: results from a Swedish tax policy in 1992". *Addiction*, 92, 859-870.

Ramstedt, M. and Hope, A. (2004) "The Irish drinking culture: Drinking and drinking-related harm; A European comparison". Dublin: Department of Health and Children.

Reilly, D., van Beurden, E., Mitchell, E., Dight, R., Scott, C. and Beard, J. (1998) "Alcohol education in licensed premises using brief intervention strategies". *Addiction*, 93, 3, 385-398.

Roberts, C., Blakey, V. and Tudor-Smith, C. (1999) "The impact of 'alcopops' on regular drinking by young people in Wales". *Drugs: education, prevention and policy*, 6, 1, 7-15.

Royal College of Psychiatrists (1986) *Alcohol: Our Favourite Drug*. London: Tavistock.

Ruggiero, V. and South, N. (1995) *Eurodrugs: Drug Use, Markets and Trafficking in Europe*. London: University College London Press.

Shanahan, C. (2003) "Some of them are drinking mixtures that would kill a horse". *Irish Examiner*, 25 May 2003.

Stockwell, T. and Crosbie, D. (2001) "Supply and demand for alcohol in Australia: relationships between industry structures, regulation and the marketplace". *International Journal of Drug Policy*, 12, 139-152.

Strategic Task Force on Alcohol (2002) *Interim Report of the Strategic Taskforce on Alcohol*. Dublin: Department of Health and Children.

Taylor, D. (2000) "The word on the street: advertising, youth culture and legitimate speech in drugs education". *Journal of Youth Studies*, 3, 3, 333-352.

Tovey, H. and Share, P. (2000) *A Sociology of Ireland*. Dublin: Gill and Macmillan.

van Ree, E. (2002) "Drugs, the democratic civilising process and the consumer society". *International Journal of Drug Policy*, 13, 349-353.

World Health Organisation (2001) *Declaration on Young People and Alcohol*. Adopted at the WHO European Ministerial Conference in Stockholm, Sweden. World Health Organisation Regional Office for Europe.

Wyn, J. and White, R. (1997) *Rethinking Youth*. London: Sage.

Debates

Chapter 7

OPEN FORUM DISCUSSION

This discussion section includes contributions from the audience as well as those who presented papers on the day of the conference (4 November 2003). Not all of those who presented at the conference have contributed chapters to this volume. The proceedings below are a combination of two separate discussion sessions. We have edited contributions only with the aim of improving their "flow", or making them easier to understand, but have been careful not to add to, or take from, the points made by contributors.

Lional Stanbrook, PRM Consultants: I appreciate what Dr Paula Mayock said right at the conclusion; that the remedies part of the issue, which is part of the subtitle of this seminar, would be dealt with in the afternoon, but I just wondered if there were any initial remarks that any of the speakers so far today would make in that category. We certainly heard a lot about reasons and ramifications but is there any possibility of a few words on possible remedies?

Luke Reaper, TNS mrbi: I suppose just in terms of listening to Dr Mayock and obviously my paper as well, a number of points come through. One just worth noting is, I suppose, the role of family and parents in today's society. How they fit in is one aspect which we need to look at. I suppose the other thing is that we have all discussed the affluent society that we live in, and that is another issue that needs to be tackled. The wider social issue of work pressure seems to have come through quite strongly as well. This is evident in terms of some of the quotations from the qualitative research [see Mayock's Chapter 6], where people talk about work pressures and how they "go out" afterwards. So in terms of talking about alcohol, in terms of its role, it appears that there are a lot of wider social issues here that we need to understand and it is quite interesting that people actually voice that continually, in terms of work pressures at the end of a week — "I am stressed out" and those sort of things.

Paula Mayock, Trinity College Dublin: I know that the National Alcohol Strategy document, the interim report, summarises very comprehensively what has been a success and what is not a success. Now, unfortunately, prevention and, for example, in the form of school-based education, ranks extremely low in that domain, albeit that we have a very captive audience in schools, in terms of delivering various programmes. What of course does come out on top are various sorts of efforts to regulate when people can start to drink, for example. It is probably true to say that we don't enforce the legal drinking age heavily enough in this country and we are quite complacent about it. Maybe even in relation to — I am not suggesting it is not a good idea for children to drink with parents — but the mrbi study did show high levels of this sort of acceptance of this in the home and maybe we are talking about their previous generations and an acceptance of alcohol as just a routine product. Unfortunately, when young people leave their home, alcohol isn't quite as routine as having a glass of wine and is being consumed in various settings for different kinds of aims and purposes. So I think that we certainly need to make a distinction perhaps between different styles of drinking and to help people, and young people in particular, to distinguish between what is obviously a more moderate and safe approach to alcohol, than say, for example, more risky patterns of heavy drinking. So I think that some of these issues could do with being looked at.

Andrew Brown, Advertising Information Group: I think what is really interesting is that young people have often got drunk, but got drunk by accident. It seems to me that there is a serious attitude shift where getting drunk by design — where that is the purpose of drinking — has occurred. This is true if you look at the attitudes here and certainly in the UK, and you compare those with Italy, for example. With kids in Italy "it is not cool to be drunk"; here there has been an attitude shift and it has resulted in behavioural change. I don't know whether that is reversible or not.

Ken Kinsella, Union of Students in Ireland: I was just wondering what the panel's view on later opening hours is? Now, my understanding and certainly my take on why hours were extended, was to move to a more continental style of drinking, whereby people would go out later and maybe drink less. However, the culture of youth in Ireland was to go to bars at 8.30 pm, and that has remained, and now as a result, it is my belief that people are drinking from 8.30 till later opening hours, till 12.30 as opposed to 11.30. I was just wondering does the panel share this view or how do they see the later opening hours?

Luke Reaper, TNS mrbi: I suppose I can see the rationale of bringing in the later opening hours. I agree with you that it does not really tackle our cultural attitude and how we drink. We talked a lot today about "how things are today", in terms of the excesses etc., but again, if you cast your mind back ten years, it is not to say that there has never been under-age drinking to a large extent. I think in terms of how we drink in this country — we do drink differently. It is not necessarily that the entry age might be different to other countries. I think we just do drink differently in terms of how we approach it and in terms of the whole culture of drinking. I think changing the opening hours will not in itself tackle the culture issue. I think it is a wider issue that needs to be explored and dealt with.

Paula Mayock, Trinity College Dublin: I suppose what I would say about opening hours is that we extended the opening hours and now we are, sort of, I suppose, in a panic to claw back, and say "let's close again at 11.30 on a Thursday". We already extended them — I think that young people view that as a form of, a desperate effort on behalf of authority figures and organisations, I guess, to address an issue. I am not sure that it is necessarily going to do anything at this stage. I think there is a fairly definite pattern set and one of the things that you pointed out yourself was that people continued — we did not achieve a continental style of drinking, through extending our hours. But neither are we going to achieve it through cutting it back now all of a sudden to 11.30.

Andrew Brown, Advertising Information Group: I agree with that. Certainly the experience in the UK, in Scotland, is that they have very restrictive licensing hours, but very high levels of drunkenness. The incidence of drunkenness declined when the hours were relaxed. Having said that, I mean if all the clubs closed at the same time you have still got everyone in the street at the same time. If there is some way of staggering closing hours, which is what they are talking about in the UK now, so that you don't have all the clubs shutting at the same time and everybody coming out into the streets and confrontations. However, I don't think it is going to affect how much people drink. In the UK again, there is now a feeling that people drink at home before they go out, because of course drinking out is expensive. So they get themselves started at an off license price and then they go out.

Malcolm MacLachlan, Trinity College Dublin: I think perhaps one of the interesting distinctions between the UK and Ireland is that, if you like, the social family unit is stronger here. But also, people here are living at home with their parents for longer. One of the consequences of this is that young people have much more disposable income than before, so more "pleasure" can be bought.

Andrew Brown, Advertising Information Group: Certainly in the UK, the major change over 20 years is the age at which people get married (if they get married at all), and the age of the arrival of the first child. They have suddenly invented another ten to fifteen years of teenage behaviour. What used to happen at the age of twenty now happens in the early thirties.

Luke Reaper, TNS mrbi: I think we talked a little about the work pressures and the social pressures as well. Society has moved on — it is quite different to a number of years ago — people do look for ways of getting out and letting off steam as well, and that is part of it, and that does come into play in terms of the level of alcohol consumption. Also, I suppose there are more young people in Ireland [compared to many other

countries]. We have to remember that in terms of the youth population —
there are a lot more of them around, so you see them a lot more as well. I
suppose the final point being that, in terms of the role of the family as
well, whereby if you looked back ten to fifteen years ago, often both partners were not working. Again, that has changed the dynamic of the family
in terms of keeping an eye on the kids, young people, whatever.

Mary Cunningham, National Youth Council: I am just interested that
20 per cent of young people are not drinking and there seems to have
been a significant body of research looking at the reasons why 80 per
cent are. Is there a parallel process that is looking at those 20 per cent
that are not, who obviously are living in the same cultural environment,
within the same context, with the same work pressures, etc. etc. and obviously getting their "buzz" in some other way?

Paula Mayock, Trinity College Dublin: No there isn't a parallel strand
of research and in fact there isn't a strand of research even for the former. We know that 80 per cent are drinking and a proportion of that 80
per cent are drinking heavily at times. We don't really know why. We
have not really gone out and asked them in a comprehensive way, in a
way that looks at different sectors of the consumer population, let's say
across age ranges. Look at school-goers first and then college goers, so
we don't know very much about either unfortunately.

Patrick Criton, An Garda Síochána: I see it, if I may borrow a phase
from economics, in terms of a supply side and a demand side, and much
of the debate at the moment circulates around the supply side. That is
natural enough because it places the onus somewhat on the drinks industry itself, but the demand side is really where a lot of this is coming from
and that, of course, is a lot more difficult. We have to find out why people decide to spend their disposal income on drink and why they will
engage in binge drinking. It is useful to go back to George Best [dis-
cussed in the introduction], I think, at this stage. We started with him and
he is highly significant because people do look up to him, they have seen
him, his particular mode of behaviour, he has shown that he was quite
successful socially. Now that can be quite significant and send a certain

signal that is picked up and he is a icon really in some respects for his activities and all his adventures have become legend. In the Garda Síochána, I am not simply being defensive in relation to some of the remarks made earlier, but we are part of the SPHE programme, which is rolling out into the secondary schools and the primary schools, along with the other Departments of Health and Education. It is a comprehensive programme with ten or eleven modules in it and it does address the whole business of drink and drug use. We have introduced the age guard system as well and in relation to enforcement issues, I think we have done a fair bit on enforcement issues but we ourselves come up against the barriers in regard to enforcement of the liquor licensing laws "down the country" [in rural areas]. It is a big issue in a good many towns. But if I may revert again to the whole business of identifying where this demand is coming from, from inside the individual's mind, I think we have to enter there. This is the most difficult one but if there was an easy answer we would not be sitting here talking about it. There isn't that easy an answer and I think it has to go back down to a determination of where the demand comes from, from the individual.

Nicola Gordon, PR@The Helme: This it not a question for Luke really, just a clarification. You said in your paper that 65 per cent of people were allowed to drink at home. I was wondering if you could define what drinking at home is. Is that having a glass of wine with dinner? Or is it letting him or her go up to their room with a group of friends?

Luke Reaper, TSN mrbi: Well, it is just what it says. It is literally just being allowed to drink at home, so it is just in general, rather than in any specific area of home, or under supervision. It is literally at home, so it is in that context the question was asked.

Patrick Carroll, Association of Secondary Teachers of Ireland: I am impressed with the speakers and the statistics which have been giving here this morning. It illustrates that we have a problem here in Ireland, but unfortunately, as with a lot of problems, like the Gardaí [police] and the teachers have been flagging these, and Dr Mick Loftus, for some years with regard to the abuse of alcohol, and nothing has been done.

Unfortunately, according to the statistics, things are getting worse from what we can see. But, unfortunately, it takes something like the murder of Veronica Guerin [the crime journalist] to focus the mind with regard to the problems, and when that happened something was done. The recent case in the Central Criminal Court where some of the witnesses said that they could not remember because they were "out of their mind" with regard to alcohol and drugs, maybe will focus the mind with regard to the problem that is here. But I would agree with Dr Mick Loftus that the media and the advertising industry have a lot to answer for here because of their focus on the new designer drinks, and I suppose designer drugs as well, that are emerging from the advertisements on television in particular.

Lynne Swinburne, National Youth Council: Just to ask, if we don't know why this 80 per cent are drinking, some to risky levels, where are these remedies coming from? I mean, are we presuming that we know the remedies without actually finding out; if we have no basis of research to say what the reasons are for the drinking, the risky drinking, are we simply presuming here?

Malcolm MacLachlan, Trinity College Dublin: I think that one of the things, for me anyway, that is coming through is the idea of the issue being multifaceted, and also of the interaction between individual responsibility and cultural encouragement, of certain consumption behaviours. Hopefully, one of the things we will be addressing this afternoon, is in fact what sort of evidence is there at those different sorts of levels, in terms of — perhaps there are levels of drinking that are OK, and there are levels that are dangerous. How do we intervene, both at individual, and hopefully, societal levels, as well? So I think that the ambiguities are real and will be there, and will probably still be there after discussing some of the remedies; I don't think we are going to find one way to solve it.

Joe Doyle, Eastern Regional Health Authority: We recently held a conference on alcohol and action, "Alcohol — Everyone's Responsibility". I feel that there is no point in blaming young people, the media or the drinks industry. We all have a responsibility in this and we published a document as a result of that conference, where we encouraged young people to drink in a moderate fashion. But the main player in helping us to do that is the parent. I feel that the real responsibility lies on parents in this issue.

Nicola Gordon, PR@The Helme: There have been a lot of developments since 2002, or at least since 2000. I mean the CCCI has been set up and then the advertising industry itself has been instrumental in banning advertising around school environments as well. So I think it is important that everyone should be, probably everyone here is, aware of that.

Fiona O'Connor, Foróige NDYO: I just want to make the comment that really when we are talking about remedies and young people and binge drinking — just the importance of working with young people on the ground — offering real positive alternatives. I think it is something that hasn't maybe been mentioned today and I think it is very, very, important to emphasise that. Organisations are working with young people, offering real alternatives and that really needs to be concentrated on, from all levels.

Malcolm MacLachlan, Trinity College Dublin: Perhaps I can throw open a question, in fact one of the ideas I kicked off with, concerns the notion of social responsibility. There is a danger of scaling things up. However, clearly the drinks industry, the advertising industry, and public health community, are all players and have different sorts of social responsibility. Who is to police "responsibility"?

Andrew Brown, Advertising Information Group: To police the problem of making sure people take various types of responsibility, that is a difficult one. I think in some senses, for instance, the advertisers are already self-policed, in some ways. Some people might not approve of them, others would approve. The question is, how you police other bits of society? Let me tell you something — someone just mentioned the banning of advertising in schools. Well I had to give a talk last year to one of Britain's most distinguished public schools, because I was thinking of sending my son there and it was a Philosophy group run by a Catholic Jesuit as it happened, and they invited me to lunch. We went to lunch and they said would you like some wine and I said "would *you* like some wine?" and they said "yes please", and this is in the school refectory, and a bottle of wine was ordered for the eight of us, and a bell went, and I thought, off they will go, but they didn't go anywhere; they stayed on. I questioned them about this and I said, was this the policy of the school? They said "yes" it was the policy of the school. It was a thing to do, it was a sophisticated thing to do. Nobody got drunk, we had about half a glass each and you see that in some sense this represents an interesting dilemma. On the one hand, the draconians say you have got to ban, you have to stop, you have to make this taboo. Well if you are a 15-year-old and adults say it is bad for you, you mustn't do it — it is the best thing you can possibly do! Whereas if you are given a model of doing it sensibly, in an adult way, then you do it that way. Now I think if you want to answer the question on education, schools have an interesting role to play, not nearly as powerful a role as parents, but how you police parents is beyond me. I don't know any way in which you can do this, except by trying to help parents to sensibly teach their children and model to their children what is going on. There are very interesting booklets which help them do this. But even in the secondary socialization thing, i.e. in schools, one could find ways, I think, of modelling and showing how this can be done to young people. I think the banning route is the precise opposite and will never have an effect, and that liberal behaviour and sensible adult behaviour is by far the best method. Now there are other groups as well, who take responsibility, and one person made an extraordinarily sensible comment about the fact that there are many people working with young people's groups and of course they have a very powerful influence on them, showing them, modelling to them, explaining to them. I think they need a lot of support. I don't think they need policing, I think they need support. It was too difficult a question and that is the best I can do.

Henk Hendriks, TNO Nutrition and Food Research Institute, Netherlands: It is very difficult to say. I think it is very important to have a balanced view on this item because it is very complex and I think we should acknowledge that there are two sides to the story. In addition to that I think it is very important to use the data in the way that it is provided and to use good data, to use the scientific evidence in a way that is available.

To be very critical of this data and to use it in a proper way so that we can, from both sides, work through a consensus model in saying, not only in effect that there is a scientific concern as to what the data show us, as well as what concerns us, in the belief that there are two sides to this story. I think it is a joint effort that should be pursued.

Cindy Dring, National University of Ireland, Galway: It has been clearly demonstrated today that it is everybody's issue. No one group bears a full responsibility. With regard to advertising, which I have been particularly concerned about, we did not suggest that advertising should be banned. This hasn't been shown to be a particularly good road to go down, although some countries have chosen to do so. It is practically impossible to do so anyway in today's global economy with satellite television and so on. For instance, sports teams wearing alcohol logo jerseys — that constitutes another type of promotion and marketing. With regard to tobacco advertising, in California (I think) the Fairness Doctrine stated that for every tobacco advertisement there should be a counter advertisement, and so on. I am not sure if it was one-to-one, I think it was so many counter-advertising types of messages for every pro-smoking message. When this happened, smoking levels went down fairly dramatically. I think also what has not been shown to work is self-monitoring and self-regulation. Nowhere has self-regulation worked. I think maybe people may be very well intentioned: there is pre-vetting of advertisements going on, but this again is by the industry itself, without involvement of health professionals and people in public health. It is essentially "a complaints based" sort of process, where if there is a complaint received about an advertisement, it is examined and the decision is made whether to pull the advertisement or not. But by this time the advertisement has already been on the air and may or may not be deemed to be breaking the codes. Codes are difficult because they are a little bit waffly, even though they have been improved somewhat. They still are open to interpretation and they don't reflect the needs of young people and that is what we have been talking about today.

Malcolm MacLachlan, Trinity College Dublin: Just to briefly summarise; one thing that has come home to me from today's discussion is that, rather than polarising the debate which I think has been the case over many years, there is quite a lot of middle ground and that middle ground is something that needs to be built on and perhaps build out towards the extremes on each side — to bring them together. I was talking jokingly before about the peace process in Ireland and how in a sense we need to have a bit of a peace process in terms of addressing this terribly important issue of binge drinking. The other aspect that is clear to me is the internationalisation of the problem. It is terribly important to include local groups, individuals, youth councils, and so on. But it is also important to include not just governments, but intergovernmental and international organisations. If you have advertisements being beamed in from all around the world, no one government is going to solve that sort of problem. By enhancing the middle ground, and by internationalising it, by getting a lot of different players involved, a pro-social platform can be built to combat the negative effects of excessive alcohol consumption. It is important to accept that some people value and enjoy drinking, but also to recognise that it can have very harmful effects when taken in excess. Whatever each of the players do, they must consider, is this a moral, an appropriate and a healthy way of pursuing our goals?

Cultivating Suicide?

Destruction of Self in a Changing Ireland

Caroline Smyth,
Malcolm MacLachlan
and Anthony Clare

ISBN 1-904148-15-8   2003   €16.50

Ireland has recently experienced unparalleled economic growth and has reached a state of prosperity that makes our European neighbours envious. In addition, with the introduction of divorce, the decline of the Catholic Church as an institution and the consequent decline in religious practice, Irish culture has changed at many levels. This change has come at a great cost, however, as can be seen in the dramatic increase in the Irish suicide rate, especially among young men. In this time of economic growth and prosperity, why are so many of Ireland's young people, at a significantly higher proportion than their European counterparts, taking their own lives? What is it about Irish culture which is either creating or contributing to such a sense of anomie and lack of hope?

This book looks at the issue of suicide in the Irish context. It takes a specifically cultural approach — as opposed to psychological or medical — by addressing two fundamental questions: "Why has there been an increase in suicide in Ireland in recent years?" and "What changes has Ireland seen that other countries have not, or have dealt with differently, which might explain why Ireland has a higher rate of suicide relative to those countries?" Included in the authors' findings will be analyses of the changing nature of the Irish family, the dramatic societal changes in the last two decades, issues concerning masculine identity and self-worth and case studies of individuals who have considered or attempted suicide. The book concludes with a look at the current suicide prevention programmes and offers specific suggestions on how they could be strengthened.